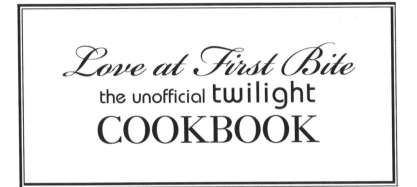

Love at First Bite
the unofficial twilight
COOKBOOK

Also by author Gina Meyers

The Magic of Bewitched Trivia and More
The Magic of Bewitched Trivia book
The Magic of Bewitched Cookbook
Love At First Bite: The Unofficial Twilight Cookbook
Bite At Twilight: Vampires, Forks, and Knives Cookbook
Life Lessons Learned From My Fortunes: Inspiration Edition
The Unofficial Twilight Trivia Book

Love at First Bite
the unofficial
twilight
COOKBOOK

GINA MEYERS

iUniverse, Inc.
New York   Bloomington

Love at First Bite
The Unofficial Twilight Cookbook

Book front and back cover concept and design by David Lawrence Meyers. Hand model for front cover, Lauren Rose Meyers. Unless otherwise noted, photos taken by Gina Meyers. All rights reserved.

iUniverse books may be ordered through booksellers or by contacting:

iUniverse
1663 Liberty Drive
Bloomington, IN 47403
www.iuniverse.com
1-800-Authors (1-800-288-4677)

Because of the dynamic nature of the Internet, any Web addresses or links contained in this book may have changed since publication and may no longer be valid. The views expressed in this work are solely those of the author and do not necessarily reflect the views of the publisher, and the publisher hereby disclaims any responsibility for them.

ISBN: 978-1-4502-2200-6 (sc)
ISBN: 978-1-4502-2201-3 (ebk)

Library of Congress Control Number: 2010905855

Printed in the United States of America

iUniverse rev. date: 04/21/2010

Contents

Introduction

The international phenomenon known as *Twilight* fever has ignited excitement in the kitchen. Delectable delights to satisfy the appetites of the humans can be found in the fictional book *Twilight. Love at First Bite: the Unofficial Twilight Cookbook* is meant to offer a satisfying array of warm, lovely dishes that anyone of any age can cook with ease and enjoyment. To help the reader determine the level of skill involved in preparing each dish, the recipes are labeled "easy", "medium", or "hard". One fork means "easy", two forks, "medium", and three forks means it is a "difficult" or "hard" recipe.

Filled with forbidden love, action, and danger, so brace yourself, and bring your very best table manners and your appetites. Don't forget your forks. Beautiful Bella Swan will be serving up some scrumptious delights to satisfy even the pickiest puritan "vegetarian" vampires. Intertwined in the pages of *Love at First Bite*, you will find Bell's Lasagna, Harry's Famous Fish Fry, Mushroom Ravioli, Blushing Bella Punch, just to name a few. Your senses will be filled deep with the sweet aroma of mouthwatering I Dare You to Eat Pizza Edward, and sinfully delicious Red Velvet Cake. You know when the rooster crows, it is time to awaken your sense of taste and take a Bite at Dawn to Lemon Blueberry cake, Plum Pecan Waffles, or Grand Slam Sundae. Red juicy ripe vine tomatoes marinated in raspberry vinaigrette tempts the taste buds and is a featured salad in the There Are Cold Cut Sandwiches in the Fridge section. Pucker up and take a long cool sip of Sparkling Honey Lemonade in a citrus salt rimmed glass, one of the virgin recipes found in the beverage chapter. Give into your epicurean temptation and take a bite into *Love at First Bite: the Unofficial Twilight Cookbook.* The recipes will leave you breathless and hungry for more.

Besides luscious recipes, you'll also find cast lists for *Twilight, New Moon,* and *Eclipse,* as well a *Twilight* Party Planning Checklist, Bella's Prom Planner, and tons of trivia. Also find invaluable resources on upcoming Unofficial *Twilight* Conventions, Twilight Cooking Classes and more.

It would be more … prudent for you not to be my friend. But, I'm tired of trying to stay away from you, Bella.-Edward

About three things I was absolutely positive. First, Edward was a vampire. Second, there was a part of him and I didn't know how dominant that part might be that thirsted for my blood. And third, I was unconditionally and irrevocably in love with him.-Bella

Bite at Dawn
(Breakfast)

Breakfast time, he said casually kidding and you said I couldn't act.
—Edward talking to Bella

Breakfast for the human, milk and cereal.
—Edward

Charlie's Fried Eggs

2 eggs
1 tablespoon butter or margarine
Salt and pepper to taste

Directions: In a skillet, melt butter or margarine over medium heat. Once the butter has melted, crack two eggs into the skillet and cook. Once the egg whites have turned white and set, about one minute per side, flip with a spatula. Salt and pepper to taste.

Eggs Benedict, photo credit, David Meyers.

Last night I'd discovered Charlie couldn't cook much besides fried eggs and bacon.

—Bella

Eggs Benedict

3 English muffins
6 slices broiled ham
6 poached eggs
Hollandaise sauce

Directions: Split and toast English muffins. Slice ham, ¼ inch in thickness and place on the English muffin halves. Top each with one egg and then smother with hollandaise sauce. Serve hot. Makes six.

Tip: Country fried potatoes and fresh fruit such as cantaloupe, strawberries, pineapple, and orange slices make excellent brunch side dishes to compliment your Eggs Benedict.

Grand Slam Sundae

2 cups of fresh, frozen, or canned peaches (in light syrup)
2 cups of low fat vanilla yogurt
1 ½ cups of fresh or frozen blackberries
¼ cup of granola cereal

Directions: Prepare fresh peaches by slicing peaches into ¼ inch thick slices and removing the peach fuzz with a serrated knife. If using frozen fruit, please defrost by following the directions found on the package insert. If using canned peaches, please drain excess liquid out of the canned peaches and disregard. Place the ingredients in four tall glasses. Prepare the Grand Slam Sundae by layering ¼ cup of the yogurt, 1/3 cup of the peaches, ¼ cup of the yogurt ¼ cup of the berries alternating between the desired fruit and the yogurt. Top the Grand Slam Sundae with granola. Makes four sundaes.

Plum Pecan Waffles

¾ cup of pecans, chopped and divided
1 ½ cups of flour
1 ½ teaspoons of baking powder
¼ teaspoon of salt
3 tablespoons of brown sugar
1 ½ cups of milk
2 eggs
1 teaspoon vanilla extract
2 tablespoons butter, melted
1 cup of plums, pitted, diced

Directions: Preheat waffle iron. Spread pecans on a baking sheet and toast in a 325 degree oven for five minutes or until lightly browned, then cool. In a medium bowl, whisk together flour, baking powder, salt and brown sugar. In a separate bowl, mix together milk, eggs, and vanilla extract. Pour approximately half of the liquid mixture into the dry ingredient mixture, whisk, then repeat. Stir in the melted butter, fold in the diced plums and ½ cup of the toasted pecans. Spray waffle iron with cooking spray and spoon batter onto the preheated waffle iron, cook until golden. Top with additional plums and pecans.

Blueberry Muffins

2 cups of all-purpose flour
2 teaspoons of baking powder
½ teaspoon salt
½ cup of butter or margarine, softened
1 cup and 1 tablespoon of sugar, divided
2 large eggs
½ cup milk
1 teaspoon vanilla extract
2 ½ cups of fresh blueberries

Directions: Heat oven to 375 degrees. Line twelve 3-inch or fourteen 2 ½ inch muffin pan cups with paper liners. Next, combine flour, baking powder and salt in a bowl. Beat butter and 1 cup of sugar in a large mixing bowl at medium speed until light and fluffy, then add eggs one at a time, beating well after each addition. Add the dry ingredients alternately with milk and vanilla extract. Begin and end with the dry ingredients, until the batter is smooth. Fold berries into the batter with a rubber spatula and divide and spoon batter into the muffin-pan cups. Sprinkle with remaining 1 tablespoon of sugar. Bake for thirty minutes or until toothpick inserted comes out clean. Cool muffins in the pan for five minutes, then remove. Makes 12 muffins.

I really missed you Bells. The food around here sucks when you're gone.- Charlie Swan

Full Moon Pancakes

2 cups of all-purpose flour
1 tablespoon of baking powder
½ teaspoon of salt
2 tablespoons of sugar
1 teaspoon of pumpkin pie spice
2 eggs
1 ¾ cups milk
3 tablespoons of melted butter, plus 1 tablespoon for frying
½ cup cooked and mashed pumpkin or canned pumpkin

Directions: Sift together the flour, baking powder, salt, sugar and pumpkin pie spice in a large bowl. In a medium bowl, whisk the eggs and milk.. Add three tablespoons ob melted butter and the pumpkin to the wet ingredients, and whisk together. Pour the mixture over the dry ingredients, and stir just until blended, a few lumps are ok. Heat the remaining butter on a griddle over medium-high heat. Pour ¼ cup of the batter for each pancake. When the pancakes bubble on top, flip with a spatula and cook until golden on the other side. Makes twenty pancakes.

Sunflower Tangerine Dream French toast

6 pieces of Sunflower bread, pre sliced (or you may use sliced sourdough)
2 teaspoons of vanilla extract
3 eggs
¼ cup of milk
Juice of three small tangerines
Maple syrup
1 tablespoon of powdered sugar (optional, sprinkled on top)

Directions: Whisk milk, eggs, juice of tangerines and vanilla in a medium bowl. Spray a 9x9 inch baking pan with cooking spray and set aside. In a large skillet, over medium-low heat melt butter or margarine. Next, coat each piece of bread evenly with the egg mixture on both sides of the bread and transfer to the skillet. Cook coated bread heating slowly until bottom is golden brown, two to four minutes and with a spatula flip the French toast and cook the other side. Serves 6. May top with syrup and powdered sugar and tangerine slices as garnish.

Sunflower Tangerine Dream French Toast,
cooking and photo credit Gina Meyers.

There Are Cold Cut Sandwiches in the Fridge

(Light Fare, Sandwiches, and Salads)

Corned Beef Sandwich

2 slices bread
Softened butter
2 slices cooked corned beef
Prepared mustard

Directions: Place corned beef between two slices of buttered bread. Add mustard to taste.

There is no law that says I can't cook in my own house.-Charlie

Club Sandwich

2 slices bread
Butter
2 slices of cold chicken, either deli sliced chicken or leftover chicken
Mayonnaise
2 strips crisp bacon
2 tomato slices

Directions: Toast bread, and spread one slice with butter and the other with mayonnaise. Sandwich the chicken, tomato, and bacon between the slices of toast.

Bella prepares grilled cheese sandwiches for her dad Charlie, Billy Black, and Jacob, Billy's son.

Jacob Black's Grilled Cheese Sandwich

Monterey Jack or cheddar cheese, thinly sliced
Margarine or butter
2 slices white or wheat bread

Directions: Spread margarine or butter on one side of each piece of bread. Place cheese between the slices of bread, unbuttered sides facing in. In a skillet over low heat, lightly brown both sides of the sandwich till the cheese is melted.

Ham and Apple Sandwich

1 tablespoon of apple butter
2 teaspoons chopped onion
1/2 teaspoon mustard
2 slices raisin bread
1 slice ham
1 slice of Cheese (provolone, Swiss, or Monterey jack), thinly sliced
1 Red apple, thinly sliced, I suggest trying Jersey Mac or Paula Red varieties for juiciness and crunch factor.

Directions: Toast the raisin bread. When the toast is cool, add mustard and onions to one slice of toast. On the other slice, place the apple butter and apple slices. Lastly, add the ham and cheese to complete the sandwich.

So I requested to be assigned kitchen detail.
—Bella describing her dad's lack of cooking skills

Tuna Sandwich

2 slices sourdough bread, toasted
1 can tuna, drained of water
1/4 cup mayonnaise
1 sweet pickle, diced
1 celery stalk, finely chopped

Directions: Mix ingredients in a bowl, and place in between the two pieces of toasted bread. There will be leftover tuna mix, enough to make two more sandwiches.

Sweet Pepper Relish

1 red bell pepper, sliced
1 orange bell pepper, sliced
1 yellow bell pepper, sliced
4 garlic cloves, minced
4 tablespoons of olive oil
Salt and pepper to taste
1 teaspoon Italian seasoning
1 cup white wine
2 tablespoons of balsamic vinegar

Directions: In a large skillet, over medium heat, heat oil and add sliced bell peppers and garlic. Sauté until bell peppers are soft. Sprinkle with salt, pepper, and seasonings. Reduce heat to low and add white wine and vinegar. Continue to cook until liquid is reduced and peppers are very tender. Serve on toasted sliced baguettes or over chicken, steak or fish. Makes six to eight servings.

Yellow Squash and Tomato Parmesan

2 yellow crookneck squash, cut into 1/2 inch slices
2 large tomatoes, cut into ½ inch slices
½ cup of grated Parmesan Cheese, divided
1 tablespoon of dried oregano
2 tablespoons of butter or margarine, melted

Directions: In an 8x8 inch baking dish, layer half the squash and tomatoes on the bottom of the baking dish. Next, sprinkle half of the Parmesan cheese and half of the dried oregano. Drizzle with melted butter or margarine. Bake in a 350 degree oven covered for thirty minutes. Top with remaining Parmesan cheese and oregano. Makes 6 servings.

> What if I'm not the hero? What if I'm the bad guy?
> —Edward

Monster Eggs

6 hard-boiled eggs
1/4 cup mayonnaise
1 teaspoon mustard
1 teaspoon red wine vinegar
Paprika to garnish

Directions: Place eggs in a large pot with enough tap water to cover the eggs by 1 inch. Bring to a rolling boil over high heat. Once the water has been brought to a rolling boil, reduce to medium heat and cook for an additional ten minutes for hard boiled eggs. Remove the eggs from the hot water. Run them under cool water. When cooled, remove shells, cut eggs in half lengthwise, and place yolks in a bowl. Mash thoroughly and then add mayonnaise, mustard, and vinegar. Stir together well. Place yolk mixture in egg whites, and sprinkle with paprika.

Tip: How to boil an egg

Place eggs in a large pot with enough tap water to cover the eggs by 1 inch. Bring to a rolling boil over high heat. Once the water has been brought to a rolling boil, reduce to medium heat and cook for an additional ten minutes for hard boiled eggs. If you are seeking a "soft boiled" egg, reduce the time by three to four minutes. Remove the eggs from the heat immediately and place the eggs under ice cold water or in a bowl of iced water to chill the "hard boiled" eggs quicker. A slightly dark greenish ring will appear on the outside of the yolk if not cooled properly. To peel the egg shell, crack on all sides and roll egg between hands to loosen shell. Please refrigerate the hard boiled eggs unless there are to be consumed within a few hours. Hard boiled eggs, kept in the shell, can be kept for up to a week in the refrigerator.

The Bella Bruscetta photo and recipe courtesy of Liz Longo.

The Bella Bruscetta

4 sausages, hot or sweet
2 cups of mushrooms
1 Loaf of Italian Bread
1 Clove of Garlic
1 cup Olive Oil
1 pound of fresh Mozzarella cheese
A dash of oregano
A dash of basil
6-8 Cherry tomatoes

Directions: Cook sausage to almost perfection in your favorite oils, add mushrooms and simmer. Slice Italian bread in four then separate top and bottom and align on a baking sheet. Drizzle olive oil over bread. Press garlic to spread over oil on bread. Once mushrooms and sausage are equally perfected, dice in bite size pieces and layer on top of bread. Sprinkle oregano. Slice your mozzarella and layer on top of sausage and mushrooms. Cut cherry tomatoes in half and place on top of the mozzarella. Place in the oven at 350-degrees for 10 minutes until mozzarella is melted to desired consistency. Take fresh basil, slip into uncooked olive oil, drip for a few seconds then set by tomatoes to top it off. Serve warm.

Will you turn into a bat?
—Bella

Like I've never heard that one before.
—Edward

Bat Chips

1 large flour tortilla
Cooking spray
Bat cookie cutter
Salt (optional)

Directions: Preheat broiler to low. Using a bat-shaped cookie cutter, press out bat shapes on the tortilla. Spray cookie sheet with cooking spray, and broil tortillas until they turn crispy and golden brown. Sprinkle with salt if desired. Depending on the size of the cookie cutter, one large flour tortilla will yield approximately four bat chips.

Salad a la Cullen

Butter lettuce, 1 head
6 Sliced strawberries
12 red grapes, halved and seeded
2 whole red apples, seeded and chopped into bite size pieces
4 ounces vanilla or lemon yogurt
¼ cup of roasted peanuts, honey roasted preferred
1 tablespoon honey
2 tablespoons vinegar
1 tablespoon olive oil
Salt and pepper to taste

Directions: For the dressing, in a salad bowl mix well the vanilla or lemon yogurt, honey, vinegar, olive oil and salt and pepper to taste. Tear the lettuce into bite size pieces and place in salad bowl. Toss to coat. Top with sliced strawberries, red grapes, and red apples, toss again to coat. Sprinkle with roasted peanuts. Serves 6.

Breaking Dawn Berry Salad

2 cups of mixed greens
½ cup each of raspberries and blackberries
½ avocado, sliced
¼ cup of red onion, sliced
2 tablespoons chopped pecans
2 tablespoons of raspberry vinaigrette

Directions: In a medium sized bowl, toss all ingredients and coat with vinaigrette dressing.

Broccoli Raisin Salad

1 purple onion, thinly sliced
1 package fresh broccoli florets
1 cup golden raisins
1 cup mayonnaise
4 bacon slices, cooked and crumbled
2 tablespoons red wine vinegar

Directions: In a salad bowl, toss all ingredients together. Allow salad to chill in the refrigerator for at least 2 hours before serving.

Tomato Salad

1 bunch of fresh spinach
1 head of Bibb lettuce
2 large ripe tomatoes cut into wedges
1 ripe avocado cut into thin slices
6-8 red cherry tomatoes (whole)
6-8 yellow pear tomatoes (halved)
¼ cup pesto

Tomato Marinade
2/3 cup of raspberry vinegar
1/3 cup of olive oil
4 tablespoons of sugar
Juice of ½ lemon

Directions: Combine all ingredients in a small bowl and whisk to dissolve sugar.. Pour marinade over tomato wedges and allow to marinate overnight in the refrigerator. To assemble the salad, wash and dry spinach and lettuce leaves, and make a bed of greens on a platter. Next, ladle the marinated tomatoes over the greens and top with avocado slices and the cherry and yellow pear tomatoes. Top salad with a dollop of pesto.

Caesar Salad

2 garlic cloves, crushed
1/2 teaspoon each salt and pepper
1 tablespoon lemon juice
1 hard-boiled egg, peeled and thinly sliced into cross-sections
1/3 cup olive oil
1 head romaine lettuce, washed and torn into bite-sized pieces
1/2 cup grated parmesan cheese
1 cup croutons (I suggest the croutons with onion and garlic flavor)

Directions: In a large salad bowl, mix garlic, salt, pepper, lemon juice, and egg. Next, add olive oil, and mix to combine. Place lettuce in the salad bowl and toss well. Lastly, add parmesan cheese and croutons. Serves four.

We call ourselves vegetarians, inside joke.

—Edward Cullen

Broccoli Salad

1 to 2 bunches of broccoli
3/4 cup raisins
1/2 cup red onions, chopped
12 slices bacon, fried and crumbled
3/4 cup nuts (cashews, peanuts, or sunflower seeds)

Dressing
1 cup mayonnaise
1/2 cup sugar
2 tablespoons red wine vinegar

Directions: Cut broccoli into small pieces and place into bowl. Combine with nuts, raisins, onion, and bacon. Mix dressing ingredients and pour over broccoli mixture. Stir together. Chill for 1 to 2 hours before serving.

Cobb Salad

1 full head of Iceberg lettuce, shredded
3 hard-boiled eggs, divided, grated
4 green onions, sliced
8 Bacon slices, cooked and crumbled
2 ½ cups of Chicken, cooked and cubed
2 Roma tomatoes, chopped finely
1 Avocado, pitted and diced small

Dressing
1/3 cup red wine vinegar
1 teaspoon salt
1/4 teaspoon pepper
1/2 teaspoon dry mustard
1/2 teaspoon sugar
1/8 teaspoon garlic powder
2/3 cup salad oil
1/4 cup crumbled blue cheese, you may prefer to make a wedge of crumbled blue cheese rather than add it to the dressing, to have it on the side.

Directions: In a medium size bowl, combine the red wine vinegar, salt, pepper, dry mustard, sugar, garlic powder, salad oil and mix. You may prefer to leave the blue cheese crumbles out of the dressing mix and instead have it on the side of the salad. Next, place the shredded lettuce in a large salad bowl and add one quarter of the dressing and toss to coat. With the hard bowl eggs, remove the yolks and grate. Also grate the egg whites, but do so separately. Arrange the yolks in the center of the bowl and surround with the egg whites on top of the shredded lettuce. Make separate wedges of onions, bacon, chicken, tomato and avocado and serve with the rest of the dressing. Chill for 1 hour in the refrigerator. Serves 4-6.

Charlie needs me. He's just all alone up there and can't cook at all.

—Bella

Chief Swan Salad

1 head lettuce, butter or iceberg washed, can be torn or cut
½ medium Red onion, sliced (optional)
½ Cucumber, peeled or scored
1 cup Swiss Cheese, cut in strips
1 cup Ham, cubed
½ cup of Radishes, sliced (optional)
2 Tomatoes, cut into wedged
3 hard-boiled eggs, cut into wedges
*1 cup Cubed salami or chicken or turkey can be used for this recipe as well

Directions: Mix all ingredients in a bowl. Add cubed salami or bologna if desired.

Lyonnaise Salade

2 strips of Bacon, cut into one-inch pieces
A handful of fresh frisee lettuce, torn into bite size pieces
1 poached egg
1 teaspoon diced red onion
Baby potatoes
1 tablespoon of Red wine vinegar
1 tablespoon sugar
1 tablespoon extra-virgin olive oil
½ teaspoon of Dijon mustard
1 slice of French or Italian bread and a little butter to make buttered croutons (1 teaspoon of butter)
Salt and pepper to taste

Directions: Sauté bacon over medium-high heat until done, about five minutes and then drain fat. It is best to drain the excess fat from the bacon by removing the bacon from the pan or skillet, blotting the extra oil from the bacon with a paper towel. Allow bacon to cool, then cut strips into one inch pieces. Next, cut a slice of French or Italian bread into cubes. Toast on medium-high heat in a small saucepan with a teaspoon of melted butter. Only stir the bread only to turn to the other side once it is toasted. Poach your egg and please review tips for how to poach an egg. Once egg is poached, please set aside. Next, Dice red onion and prepare salad dressing. In a small jar, mix the olive oil, vinegar, mustard, salt and pepper. On a salad plate, arrange the washed frisee salad (that has been torn into bite size pieces) and add the bacon, onions, and croutons. Top with poached egg and pour dressing over the salad. Please see tip on how to make the salad dressing. Serve one.

Tip: How to poach an egg

Crack the egg and empty the contents of the shell into a small bowl. Pour 4 inches of water into a pan, and over medium heat, bring the water to a boil. Stir the water in a circular motion, then drop the egg into the middle of the swirl of water. Turn down the heat slightly and cook three to five minutes. Use a slotted spoon to remove the egg and place it on a plate. Tip:

 Tip: How to make salad dressing

In a small jar, mix the olive oil, vinegar, mustard, salt and pepper.

Lobster Salad

Iceberg lettuce, cut into bite size pieces
2 tomatoes, cut into wedges
1 pound Lobster meat
1 cup chopped celery
2 hard-boiled eggs, chopped
1/2 cup mayonnaise
2 teaspoons lemon juice
1 teaspoon ketchup
1/2 teaspoon sugar
1/4 teaspoon salt

Directions: Combine lobster, celery, and eggs in a bowl. Mix the next five dressing ingredients together well, and pour over lobster mixture. Place lobster mixture on a bed of lettuce. Garnish with tomato wedges on the side.

Artichoke Cheese Squares

2 jars (6.5 ounces) marinated artichoke hearts
1 small onion, finely chopped
1 clove garlic, chopped
4 eggs
1/4 cup bread crumbs
1/4 teaspoon each salt, pepper, and oregano
1/8 teaspoon Tabasco sauce
2 cups shredded sharp cheddar cheese
1 teaspoon of parsley, optional

Directions: Mix all ingredients together and transfer into a greased 7- by 11-inch glass baking pan. Bake at 325° for 30 minutes.

Yellow Squash and Tomato Parmesan

2 yellow crookneck squash, cut into 1/2 inch slices
2 large tomatoes, cut into ½ inch slices
½ cup of grated Parmesan Cheese, divided
1 tablespoon of dried oregano
2 tablespoons of butter or margarine, melted

Directions: In an 8x8 inch baking dish, layer half the squash and tomatoes on the bottom of the baking dish. Next, sprinkle half of the Parmesan cheese and half of the dried oregano. Drizzle with melted butter or margarine. Bake in a 350 degree oven covered for thirty minutes. Top with remaining Parmesan cheese and oregano. Makes 6 servings.

Bite Bella Bagel Bites

20 small (miniature bagels)
1 cup shredded mozzarella cheese
1/2 cup pepperoni finely cut
1 cup pizza sauce
Salt and pepper to taste
Oregano or Italian seasoning to taste

Directions: Cut bagels in half and place on a large baking sheet. Next, place the pizza sauce on each of the bagel halves, and then add cheese and pepperoni, and season to taste. Place in a 350° oven for 15 to 20 minutes or until toasted and the cheese is melted.

Twilight Time for a Party Dip

1 can (30 ounces) of refried beans
1 package of Taco Seasoning
1 container (16 ounces) of Sour Cream
1 can (3 ounces) sliced black olives
1 container (12 ounces) of prepared guacamole
½ cup of yellow onion, chopped
3 vine ripe tomatoes, chopped
3 cups shredded Cheddar Cheese

Directions: In a large bowl, mix beans and taco seasoning. Ayer beans in the bottom of a 9 x 13 inch pan. Follow with layer of sour cream, olives, guacamole, onion, tomatoes, and lastly, shredded cheese. Serve with tortilla chips. Makes 10 servings.

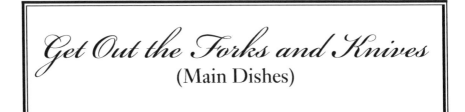

Get Out the Forks and Knives
(Main Dishes)

Bella left Charlie a note on the table explaining again where to find dinner.

Stir-Fry ala Swan

1/2 tablespoon vegetable oil
1 tablespoon sugar
1 pound lean hamburger
2 teaspoons minced garlic
1 medium onion, diced
1 medium head cabbage, shredded or cut into slightly larger than bite-size pieces
1 (10 3/4 ounce) can tomato soup
1 (8 ounce) can tomato sauce
1/4 cup water
1 tablespoon soy sauce and 1 teaspoon salt (both optional)

Directions: Heat vegetable oil in a skillet over medium heat. Add sugar, hamburger meat, onion, and garlic. With a spatula, break meat apart, and heat uncovered, stirring occasionally, until thoroughly cooked. Once the meat is browned, take it off the burner and scoop it onto a plate lined with paper towels, to remove the excess fat. Wash the skillet out with lukewarm water and then place the cooked meat along with garlic and onion, back in the skillet. Add the cabbage, tomato soup, ¼ cup of water, and tomato sauce (and salt and soy sauce, if desired). Cook covered over low heat until cabbage is tender, about 20 minutes. Makes six to eight servings. This can be complemented with white or brown rice.

Tip: To remove excess oil from browned meat, scoop onto a plate lined with paper towels. This will absorb the excess fat.

Charlie came home with a large catch.
—Bella

Charlie's Catch of the Day Crab Cakes

1 egg
3 tablespoons mayonnaise
4 teaspoons lemon juice
1/8 teaspoon red pepper flakes
1 teaspoon dried tarragon
1 tablespoon minced green onions
8 ounces crabmeat
1 tablespoon butter
10-12 Round crackers, such as Ritz name brand, broken up into cracker crumbs

Directions: In a medium bowl, whisk together egg, mayonnaise, lemon juice, red pepper flakes, tarragon, and green onions. Gently stir in the crabmeat and then mix in cracker crumbs. Next, melt butter in a skillet over medium heat. Form crab mixture into patties and place in the skillet. Fry on both sides until the patties are golden brown. Makes about four crab cakes, depending upon the size of the patties.

And so the lion fell in love with the lamb.

Lion and the Lamb Stew

2 1/2 pounds boneless lamb, cut into bite-size pieces
1/3 cup flour
2 1/2 teaspoons salt
1/4 teaspoon pepper
1/4 cup butter
1 medium yellow onion, quartered
1 clove garlic, minced
8 whole mushrooms
12 medium yellow onions (1 ¼ pounds)
1 teaspoon of sugar
1 1/4 teaspoons dried thyme leaves
2 sprigs parsley
1 large bay leaf
1 1/2 cups red wine
6 to 8 carrots, peeled (about 1 pound)
8 small new potatoes (about 1 ¼ pounds)
Chopped parsley (optional)

Directions: Blot lamb with paper towels. Trim fat from lamb and cut meat into bite-size pieces. Next, combine flour, salt, and pepper; coat the lamb evenly with the flour mixture. Reserve any excess flour. Melt butter in a Dutch oven on medium setting or large saucepan; add the floured lamb pieces, quartered onion, and garlic. Cook until lamb is browned on all sides, stirring frequently. Add remaining ingredients and bring to a boil. Reduce heat, cover, and simmer for about 1 hour, or until lamb is tender.

In Depth Directions: Wipe lamb with paper towels. Combine flour, salt and pepper, coating lamb evenly with mixture. Reserve the leftover flour. Brown lamb in hot butter in a 6 quart Dutch oven along with quartered onion and garlic, takes about ½ hour. Add more butter if needed. Remove meat as browned, add onions, mushrooms and sugar to the drippings, cook covered for about five minutes, or until lightly browned. Return lamb to pan, add thyme, parsley and bay leaf. Toss with drippings. Stir in two cups water and 1 cup of wine. Place a large sheet of waxed paper over top of Dutch oven. Place lid over the wax paper, letting it hang over. Bring to a boil. Reduce heat, simmer, covered for forty minutes. Meanwhile, pare carrots, cut each into three pieces. Scrub potatoes, pare a 1 inch band of skin from center of each. Add carrots and potatoes to the lamb, stir and combine. Bring back to a boil, reduce heat, simmer, covered for another forty minutes until tender. Remove from heat and skim away any fat from surface, combine reserved four mixture and ½ cup of red wine. Stir into liquid in the Dutch oven. Simmer, covered for an additional ten minutes. Sprinkle with chopped parsley. Serves 8.

There was fish marinating for dinner, with salad and bread left over from the night before.

Harry's Famous Fish Fry

4 cups cooked rice
About 2 pounds fresh fish fillets, such as filet of sole, whitefish, or salmon filets
3 or 4 green onions, sliced, including green parts
5 to 7 fresh mushrooms
2 medium zucchini
¼ cup of Lemon juice
2 cups sauce, cooled slightly
Parchment paper or aluminum foil

Harry's Secret Sauce
1 (14.5-ounce) can chicken broth
1/2 cup dry white wine
1/4 cup cornstarch, mixed with 1/4 cup cold water
2 tablespoon grated Swiss cheese
2 tablespoons grated parmesan cheese

HARD

Directions: In a medium-sized saucepan, heat chicken broth and wine over high heat, stirring in approximately half of the cornstarch mixture. While continuing to stir, cook the mixture until it thickens; reduce heat to low and then add the seasonings. Let cool slightly before assembling the fish packets.

The assembly of the packets starts with four 18- by 15-inch sheets of parchment (or aluminum foil). Fold each sheet in half to make 9- by 15-inch pouch. Place one-fourth of each of the ingredients—rice, green onion, mushrooms, fish, other veggies, lemon juice, and Harry's secret sauce—into each pouch. Seal and place packets on a baking sheet in a 425° oven for 20 minutes.

Kevin, you are such a gourmand.-Pam, The Office TV Show

I cooked my way through Julia Child's Cookbook and now I am half way through the Twilight Cookbook. Last night, I cooked Edward's Cornflake Chicken. -Kevin Malone, The Office TV Show

Edward's Cornflake Chicken

1 cut up chicken, washed
3 cups of cornflakes, crumbled
¼ cup of vegetable oil
Salt and pepper to taste

Directions: Heat oven to 425 degrees. Remove skin and rinse and dry chicken. In a medium size pan, pour oil and dip chicken in oil. Roll in crumbs, shake off excess and let chicken set briefly. Place cornflake chicken on a rack in a baking pan. Bake for forty five minutes, uncovered.

Charlie seemed suspicious when he came home and smelled the green peppers.

—Bella

Bella thinks about Edward as she prepares chicken enchiladas for dinner.

Chicken Enchiladas, cooking and photo credit David Meyers.

Chicken Enchiladas

1 1/2 cups enchilada sauce
1 1/4 cups stewed tomatoes
1/4 cup chopped green chilies, drained
3 cups shredded chicken, cooked beforehand
1 medium onion, finely diced
1 teaspoon of chili powder
1 teaspoon of ground cumin

1/2 teaspoon of pepper
1 cup shredding cheddar cheese
5 to 7 corn and flour tortillas

2 1/2 cups tomato sauce
2 tablespoons oil
1 tablespoon ground cumin
3/4 teaspoon chili powder
1/2 teaspoon of pepper
1/2 large green pepper, finely diced

Directions: Combine and simmer for fifteen minutes.
Brush inside of tortilla with two tablespoons of enchilada sauce; top each tortilla with 3 to 4 tablespoons of chicken mixture. Mix shredded cheese and place inside of tortilla. Roll up the tortilla and place in a baking dish, 2-Quart. Pour the remaining enchilada sauce over the tortilla mixture, including the remaining cheese. Bake 20 to 25 minutes in a 350° oven.

He was brave enough to take the first bite and he seemed to like the chicken enchiladas.

—Bella talking about her dad Charlie

Cheese Enchiladas

1/4 cup chopped onion
1 tablespoon butter
2 cups Monterey jack cheese, shredded
1 pound white cheddar cheese, shredded
2 tablespoon chopped black olives
2 tablespoons finely diced jalapeno peppers
1 teaspoon salt
12 corn tortillas

Directions: Cook onion in butter until tender in a frying pan on medium heat. In a separate skillet, over high heat fry tortillas in oil for 2 to 3 seconds on both sides with a spatula and then place on paper towels to drain excess oil, and repeat for each tortilla. Add cheese, olives, jalapenos, and seasonings to the tortillas and fold in half. Place in a greased 2 quart baking dish, 11x7 x1.5 inches, and bake at 350° for 20 minutes or until cheese has melted. Add Enchilada Sauce to taste.

Enchilada Casserole

1 ½ pounds of ground meat
1 large onion, chopped
1 clove of garlic, smashed
2 cans (8.3 ounces) of sliced olives
½ teaspoon of onion salt
½ pound of grated Cheddar cheese
6 to 8 corn tortillas

Sauce
1 large can (15 ounce) of tomato sauce with onion
1 can (10 ounce) of enchilada sauce
1 cup of water (added to the sauce, if needed)

Directions: Brown meat, onion, and garlic. Add the olives, alt and ½ cup of the sauce. Layer tortillas, dipped in sauce and meat mixture and cheese. Pour remaining sauce over and top off with cheese. Bake is a 2 quart baking dish in a 350 degree oven for 35 minutes.

I hurried downstairs to take the potatoes out and put the steak in the broil.

—Bella

Steak and Potatoes

1 (2 pound) beef brisket
1 bottle, (18 ounces) BBQ sauce
1 tablespoon garlic powder
3 tablespoons paprika
2 teaspoons brown sugar
2 teaspoons onion powder
2 teaspoons black pepper
2 teaspoons chili powder
3 to 5 potatoes

Directions: Rub seasoning on brisket and place in a Crock-Pot; cover with BBQ sauce and cook covered on low for 8 hours. Makes 4 to 6 servings. In a separate Crock-Pot, wrap washed potatoes in aluminum foil and leave in the crock pot on medium for approximately four hours. Or, you may scrub potatoes, poke a few holes in them with a fork, and rub with a little vegetable oil or wrap them in aluminum foil, and place in a 350° oven for about an hour, on a rack.

I told them not to do this.-Edward (talking about the vampire clan Cullen's cooking for Bella)

"I dare you to eat Pizza!" Pie

1(9 inch) piecrust, unbaked
4 cups of firm tomatoes, sliced
1 teaspoon of dried basil
Salt and pepper to taste
1/3 cup of mayonnaise
1/3 cup of Parmesan Cheese, shredded
1 large garlic clove, minced

Directions: Place prepared pie crust in a pie dish, bake at 450 degrees for five minutes, be careful not to over bake. Next, layer sliced tomatoes onto crust, sprinkle with seasonings.. Mix mayonnaise and cheese and garlic in a small bowl and spread over tomatoes. Return to oven and bake at 350 degrees for 35 minutes until hot and bubbly. Serves six.

Cascade Mountain Mashed Potatoes

3 pounds potatoes, peeled and cut into 1 1/2-inch pieces (about 8 large Russet potatoes)
3/4 cup milk
1 (7-ounce) can of chipotle pepper sauce, please see below recipe
Salt and pepper to taste

Chipotle Pepper Sauce Recipe
2 tablespoons of flour
2 ounces Monterey Jack Cheese
1 cup of Sour Cream
3 chipotle chilies, chopped
1 tablespoon of chicken base
2 cups of heavy cream

Directions: Melt the butter in a saucepan over low heat, then add flour and stir for 1 minute. Next, add cream and chicken base and stir until the mixture thickens. Add chilies and cheese. Stir until the cheese melts. Remove from heat. When the boiling stops, fold in the sour cream.

Directions: Place potatoes in a large stockpot and cover with water; bring to a boil over medium-high heat. Reduce heat slightly and cook potatoes until tender. Drain. Add milk and chipotle sauce to potatoes and mash. Season with salt and pepper. Makes 6 to 8 servings.

I feel just horrible, leaving you to cook for yourself, it's practically criminal negligence. You could arrest me.
-Bella

Bella's Instant Mashed Potatoes

4 cups chopped white potatoes
1/4 cup low-fat milk
Minced garlic
2 tablespoons cream cheese or grated cheddar cheese
1/2 teaspoon salt
1/8 teaspoon pepper

Directions: Peel and cut potatoes, and place in a saucepan with water. Bring to a boil over medium-high heat and then reduce the heat to low. Cook for 20 minutes or until soft. Once the potatoes are cooked, drain the water. Add milk, garlic, cheese, salt, and pepper. Mash the ingredients with an electric mixer for about three minutes. Serve warm.

Pot Roast with vegetables

4 to 5 pound pot roast (chuck, round, shoulder or rump roast)
Flour
Salt
Pepper
1 teaspoon of sugar
1/2 cup water
1 package onion soup mix
5 to 7 mini carrots
4 to 5 pearl onions
5 to 7 whole new small potatoes

Directions: Place roast in a deep pot with a lid. Dredge roast with flour, and season with salt, pepper, and sugar (for browning). Grease pan lightly. Over high heat, brown roast well on all sides (will take about 30 minutes). Once dark brown, place rack under the roast. Add 1 cup of water and package of onion soup mix. Cover and reduce heat; cook very slowly for 2 hours. Next, add small whole potatoes, pearl onions, and small carrots to the pot, and coat veggies with the onion soup mix. Continue cooking for an additional hour. Serves 8 to 10.

Irritated Grizzly Bear Steaks.
Photo credit, Gina Meyers; barbequing credit, David Meyers.

I wasn't hunting for food. I was actually trying my hand
at, tracking. I'm not very good at it.-Edward

Irritated Grizzly Bear Steaks

Beef tri-tip, 2 pounds
1/2 teaspoon chili powder
1/2 teaspoon paprika
1/2 teaspoon cumin
1/4 teaspoon garlic powder
1/4 teaspoon onion powder

Directions: Rub seasonings on tri-tip and refrigerate until ready to
grill. On a barbeque grill, roast over medium heat, turning occasionally,
about 35 minutes. Carve tri-tip into slices. Makes 4 to 6 servings.

What's for dinner?

—Charlie (Charlie asked Bella warily, partially due to the fact that, according to Bella, her mother was an imaginative cook; her experiments, however, weren't always edible.)

Charlie's Dinner in a Skillet

1 package hot dogs, sliced into 1/4-inch pieces
4 potatoes, peeled and cubed
1 green pepper, sliced
1/4 cup diced red onion
Vegetable or olive oil

Directions: In a skillet, over medium heat, add 2 to 3 tablespoons of oil. When warm, add the hot dogs, potatoes, green pepper, and onion. Sauté the ingredients until hot dogs are browned and potatoes are cooked. May add 2 to 3 tablespoons of water and reduce heat, if necessary.

Arizona Corn Bake

1 pound ground beef
2 (14.5-ounce) cans diced tomatoes
1 (15-ounce) can corn, drained
1 tablespoon chili powder
1 package corn muffin mix, mixed according to package instructions

Directions: In a skillet, over medium-high brown meat; drain. Next, add the canned tomatoes and corn as well as chili powder. Season to taste with salt and pepper. Pour into a 2-quart baking dish. Prepare the muffin mix according to the package directions. Spread the muffin mixture evenly over the cooked meat, and bake at 400° for 25 minutes or until golden.

The closest edible Mexican food was probably in Southern, California.

—Bella

Taco Soup

1 1/2 pounds hamburger
Salt and pepper to taste
1 tablespoon onion flakes
1 can, (15.25 ounces) corn, not drained
1 can, (15 ounces) kidney beans, not drained
1 can, (15 ounces) of garbanzo beans, not drained
1 large can, (14 ounces) of Mexican or Italian stewed tomatoes
1 can (10.75 ounces) tomato soup
1 package taco seasoning mix

Directions: Cook the hamburger meat until browned; drain and add salt, pepper, and onion flakes. In a large pot, combine corn, kidney beans, stewed tomatoes, tomato soup, and use the tomato soup can and place tap water in a pot with the taco seasoning mix. Add the cooked hamburger meat and bring to a simmer. Cook for 45 minutes.

Beef Stew

4 tablespoons oil
1 cup burgundy wine
1 clove garlic, crushed
1 (10-ounce) can beef consommé
2 large onions, sliced
1 (10-ounce) package frozen artichoke hearts
1 tablespoons butter
1 1/2 teaspoons salt
1/4 teaspoon pepper
18 fresh mushrooms, halved
2 1/2 pounds stew beef
1/2 teaspoon dill weed
1 package of Refrigerated biscuit dough, prepared ahead according to package directions.

Directions: Brown beef in oil, over medium high heat until meat is cooked thoroughly. Place beef mixture, as well as dill weed, wine, onions, garlic, salt and pepper and consommé, in a pot that has a tight-fitting lid. Simmer for 1 1/2 hours on medium heat or until tender. Sauté artichokes and mushrooms in butter and add to meat; simmer an additional 20 minutes. Remove from heat. Top with biscuits, and brush biscuits with butter and sprinkle with parmesan cheese.

Mom is an unpredictable cook.
—Bella talking about her mother

South of the Phoenix Border Casserole

1 pound lean beef
1/2 cup chopped yellow or white onion
2 (8-ounce) cans tomato sauce
1 tablespoon chili powder
1 teaspoon salt
1 dozen flour or corn tortillas
2 cups of Cheddar cheese, shredded

Directions: Brown meat and onions in a skillet over medium-high heat cook ground beef until no longer pink, so check to make sure meat is cooked thoroughly. Stir in the tomato sauce and seasonings. In a 2-quart glass casserole dish, alternate layers of meat, tortillas, and cheese, and bake for 20 minutes in a 325° oven.

Forks was literally, my personal hell on earth.

—Bella

You'll Need to Get out the Forks Baked Beans

2 cups uncooked navy beans, sorted and cleaned
1/2 pound cooked bacon
1 onion, finely diced
3 tablespoons molasses
2 teaspoons salt
1/4 teaspoon black pepper
1/4 teaspoon dry mustard
1/2 cup ketchup
1 tablespoon of Worcestershire sauce
1/4 cup of brown sugar

Directions: Place uncooked navy beans in a large pot with 6 cups of water and 1 tablespoon of oil. Boil gently in the large pot for 1 hour with the lid slightly titled, add hot water as needed to keep beans covered with liquid. Cook beans until tender. After rinsing beans and checking them for stones, soak them overnight in cold water. The next day, using the same water used to soak, simmer the beans in a pot for about 1 hour to 1 ½ hours. Once beans are cooked and cooled, arrange beans in a bean pot or a casserole dish, placing a portion of the beans in the bottom of the dish and then layering them with bacon and onion. Next, in a saucepan, combine the molasses, salt, pepper, ketchup, mustard, brown sugar, and Worcestershire sauce. Mix and bring the mixture to a boil and then pour over the beans. Cover the casserole dish and bake for 3 hours in a 325° oven. Cook until beans are tender; add more liquid if needed.

Tip: When dried beans boil, a foam forms on the top of the cooking liquid, this foam is a water-soluble protein released from the beans. It will be absorbed back into the bean cooking liquid. You do not need to remove the foam, however, in order to keep the foam down while cooking beans, add 1 tablespoon of butter. The best cookware to use is stainless steel or a cast iron.

Melt in Your Mouth Coq au Vin.
Photo and cooking credit, David Meyers.

Melt in Your Mouth Coq au Vin

2 boneless, skinless chicken breasts
Salt and pepper to taste
1/3 cup butter
1 1/2 cups sliced fresh mushrooms
1/4 cup white burgundy wine
2 tablespoons orange juice
1 teaspoon grated orange rind, fresh or dried whichever you have on hand.
1 (10.5-ounce) can cream of chicken soup

Directions: Sprinkle chicken breasts with salt and pepper. Heat butter in a skillet and brown chicken on both sides on medium heat setting. Add mushrooms and sauté. Add remaining ingredients and simmer until chicken is cooked, about 20 minutes. Serve with white rice.

Chow Bella
(Flavorful Italian Dishes)

Mushroom Ravioli. Photo and cooking credit, Gina Meyers.

Just eat Bella.
—Edward

Mushroom Ravioli

10 ounces mushroom ravioli or cheese-filled ravioli
2 tablespoons olive oil
2 ounces shiitake mushrooms, sliced
4 ounces button (table) mushrooms, sliced
1 clove garlic, minced
1/4 cup brandy
1 cup heavy cream
1/2 teaspoon nutmeg
Salt and pepper
1/2 cup grated parmesan cheese

Directions: Prepare ravioli according to package directions; drain. Next, over medium heat, pour olive oil in a skillet and cook mushrooms until tender. Add garlic and brandy, and cook for 2 minutes. Slowly stir in heavy cream and bring to a simmer. Season with nutmeg, salt, and pepper. When cream has thickened, stir in 1/4 cup of parmesan cheese. Then, stir in cooked ravioli, and gently simmer for 1 to 2 minutes. Serve with parmesan, garlic bread, and salad. Makes 2 servings.

Tallerina, photo by, David Meyers, cooking credit to Gina Meyers.

Tallerina

3 tablespoons shortening
1 onion, minced
1 pound ground round
1 can, (26 ounce) tomato soup
1 (15-ounce) can tomato sauce
1 cup cold water
2 tablespoons salt
2 cups uncooked broad egg noodles
2 cups canned corn
1 can, (6 ounce) ripe pitted olives
1 cup grated cheddar cheese
1 can, (4 ounces) mushrooms, pieces and stems preferred.

Directions: Melt shortening in a large pot on medium; add onions and cook until brown. Next, add meat and cook thoroughly. Add tomato soup, tomato sauce, noodles, water, and salt. Cover and cook over low heat for 10 minutes. Remove pot from stove and add corn, mushrooms, and part of the cheddar cheese. Stir and then pour mixture into a baking dish 1 x 8 ½ inches. Cover with remaining cheese, and bake at 350° for 50 minutes.

Zucchini Relleno

1 1/4 pounds zucchini, cubed
4 eggs
1/2 cup milk
1 pound Monterey jack cheese, cubed
2 teaspoon baking powder
3 tablespoons flour
2 tablespoons parsley flakes
1 small can diced green chilies
1/2 stick of butter or margarine
1/2 cup of dry bread crumbs
Salt and pepper to taste
Cooking spray

Directions: Boil squash for five minutes and then drain and cool. Next, blend eggs, milk, and all of the dry ingredients, except bread crumbs. Spray a 9- by 9-inch pan with cooking spray and then sprinkle with bread crumbs. Layer three layers, first the squash, then the chilies and lastly, the cheese. Pour liquid mixture over the squash layers and top with cut up butter or margarine pieces. Bake at 350° for 35 minutes or until set. Cut into squares and serve as an appetizer.

Pasta with Creamy Garlic and Walnut Sauce

1 1/2 cups heavy cream
1 cup walnuts
3/4 cup shredded Romano cheese
2 garlic cloves, peeled
1 teaspoon salt
1/2 teaspoon ground black pepper
1 pound bow tie–shaped pasta

Directions: Place cream, walnuts, cheese, salt, pepper, and garlic into a food processor, and blend until mixture is smooth. Cook pasta according to the package directions and drain. Toss pasta with the sauce, and return to a pan to heat the sauce. Garnish with cilantro and additional walnuts, if desired.

Tip: Candied walnuts give the pasta a little sweet kick.

Veal Scaloppini

2 1/2 pounds boned veal shoulder
1/2 cup flour
2 teaspoons salt
1/4 teaspoon pepper
1/2 cup minced onion
1/2 cup vegetable oil
3/4 cup sliced fresh mushrooms
1 3/4 cups tomato juice or strained tomatoes
1 teaspoon sugar

Directions: Cut veal into 1 1/2-inch cubes. Roll the cubes lightly in flour combined with 1/2 teaspoon of salt and 1/8 teaspoon of pepper (or a dash of salt and pepper, to taste). In a skillet, over medium heat, sauté onion in hot vegetable oil. Once the onion is browned, remove it from the skillet and place it in a 2-quart casserole dish. Next, place floured veal in the same skillet and brown on all sides. Add mushrooms, tomatoes, sugar, remaining salt and pepper. Cover and bake at 350° for 1 1/2 hours or until tender.

Bella, we are making Italiano for you.-Esme

Chicken Cacciatore

3 pound whole fryer chicken, cut into pieces and washed
1/2 cup oil
¼ cup of flour, for dredging
Garlic salt to taste
2 tablespoons chopped parsley
1 clove garlic
1 pinch thyme
2 leaves sage
1 sprig rosemary
1 small can Italian stewed tomatoes, chopped
1 small can tomato sauce
1 jar (4.5 ounces) button mushrooms, drained

Directions: Cut and wash chicken pieces. Dredge the washed chicken pieces in flour to coat lightly. In a deep frying pan, heat the oil over a medium-high flame. Add cut pieces of chicken, sprinkled with garlic salt, and cook until chicken has browned. Once browned, add the herbs and spices, as well as the tomato sauce, chopped tomatoes, and mushrooms. Cook on high heat for 30 minutes.

I Dare You to Eat Pizza, Edward.
Photo credit, Gina Meyers; cooking credit, Lucas Meyers.

I Dare You to Eat Pizza, Edward.
Photo and cooking credit, Gina Meyers.

I Dare You to Eat Pizza, Edward

English muffins
Pizza or spaghetti sauce
Mozzarella cheese
Pineapple chunks
Pepperoni
Black olives
Green pepper
Fresh sliced mushrooms

Directions: Slice all of the ingredients into bite-sized pieces, and grate the mozzarella cheese. Spread pizza or spaghetti sauce on English muffins, and add cheese and your favorite toppings. Place the pizzas on a cookie sheet, and bake at 350° for 6 minutes or until cheese is melted.

People can't smell blood.-Edward Cullen

Pasta with Broccoli and Artichokes

1 pound bow tie pasta
1 bunch of Broccoli halved
8-10 Pepperoni, cut into 1-inch strips
1 jar , (6.5 ounces) Marinated artichoke hearts, diced
1/2 cup sun-dried tomatoes
3 green onions, chopped
1 tablespoon red wine vinegar
1/4 teaspoon salt
1/4 teaspoon pepper
1/4 cup parmesan cheese

Directions: Cook pasta in lightly salted water for 10 minutes or until almost tender. Add broccoli to boiling water during the last 5 minutes of cooking and then drain. Add the cooked pasta and broccoli to a bowl along with the other ingredients, and toss. Serve hot or cold. Parmesan cheese as a topping is optional.

Tip: If you do not have bow tie pasta on hand, using angel hair pasta or spaghetti noodles will work for this recipe.

Stuffed Bella Peppers photo and cooking credit, Gina Meyers.

Stuffed Bella Peppers

1 pound of lean ground beef
1 package (10 ounces) frozen spinach, thawed and squeezed dry
1 egg or ¼ cup of egg substitute
2 cups of rice
1 cup of shredded cheddar cheese
4 red bell peppers
1 can (14 ounces) tomato sauce

Directions: in a skillet, brown beef, drain. Place spinach, beef, egg, and rice into a large bowl and mix well with a spoon. Next, add cheddar cheese and mix, then set aside. Wash and clean bell peppers, cutting off tops of peppers, and cleaning out the insides. Spoon rice mixture into peppers, top with tomato sauce. Cover and bake in a 350 degree oven for thirty minutes or until bell peppers are slightly tender. Serves 4.

Is she even Italian?-Rosalie

Her name is Bella.-Emmett

Spaghettini Primavera

4 tablespoons olive oil
1 pound sweet Italian sausage links
2 dried hot chili peppers
1 (28-ounce) can Italian plum tomatoes, drained and diced
1 cup finely minced parsley
2 large garlic cloves, minced
3 red bell peppers, peeled, seeded, and thinly sliced
1 sprig fresh oregano or 1 teaspoon dried oregano
Salt and pepper to taste
3/4 pound spaghettini
3 tablespoons finely minced parsley (as garnish, optional)
3 tablespoons parmesan cheese

Directions: Heat two tablespoons of olive oil in a large skillet over medium heat. Add sausage; cover and cook until browned on all sides. This will take about 20 minutes or so. Next, in the same skillet, heat more oil over medium-high heat. Add the chili peppers and sauté until skins turn black. Take the chili peppers out of the oil once they are cooked and discard; then add the tomatoes, parsley, and garlic to the skillet, and bring to a simmer. Reduce the heat and add the bell pepper and oregano; salt and pepper to taste. Cover and simmer for about 10 minutes. Cook the spaghettini according to package directions and drain the water. Slice the sausage and add to a large bowl along with all of the other ingredients. Top with minced parsley (as garnish) and sprinkle with parmesan cheese. Serve with garlic bread or toasted french bread.

Charlie seemed absentminded at dinner.
—Bella

It was fun to watch as he slowly began trusting me in the kitchen.
—Bella

Bells' Lasagna

1 (15-ounce) container ricotta cheese
1 egg
1 (8 ounce) package shredded mozzarella cheese
1/3 cup parmesan cheese
1 (28-ounce) jar spaghetti sauce
1 (8-ounce) can tomato sauce
Half of a 16-ounce box lasagna noodles, cooked according to package instructions
Optional: 1 box of frozen chopped spinach, 1 cup of sliced fresh mushrooms, or 1 cup shredded zucchini
Spices to season with: basil, oregano, garlic, and parsley.

Directions: Preheat oven to 350°. In a bowl, combine egg and seasonings with ricotta, parmesan, and mozzarella cheeses, and mix well. Next, spray the bottom of a 9- by 13-inch pan with cooking spray. Add a layer of noodles and then start layering with the ricotta mixture, spaghetti sauce, tomato sauce, and remaining noodles. (Optional ingredients may be added at this time as well.) Cover with aluminum foil and bake for 75 minutes. Allow to cool 10 to 15 minutes before serving.

He looks at you like you're something to eat.
—Mike

Easy Chicken Swan Parmesan

4-6 boneless chicken breasts, washed and pounded to 1/2-inch thickness (or purchase thin chicken filets)
1 egg
1/2 cup milk
Italian-seasoned bread crumbs
8 slices mozzarella cheese
1 jar , (25 ounces) spaghetti sauce (any flavor)
Parmesan cheese to taste
Salt and pepper to taste

Directions: With a fork, mix egg and milk together in a dish large enough to fit one chicken breast, and add a dash of salt and pepper. Dip washed chicken breasts into the egg and milk mixture and then into the bread crumbs. Place the chicken in a glass baking dish and pour 1 jar of spaghetti sauce over top. Next, cover with mozzarella slices and parmesan cheese, and bake for 30 minutes in a 350° oven. Make sure chicken is no longer pink in the middle by cutting a center piece to check for doneness. Serve with garlic bread and a salad or a side of green beans.

Bite at Twilight
(Desserts)

I saw Emmett grin at Mike over the food table, the red lights gleaming off his teeth, and watched Mike take an automatic step back.-Bella

Time for Tea Cake Cookies

1/2 cup margarine
3/4 cup confectioner's sugar (powdered sugar)
1 tablespoon vanilla extract
1 1/2 cups flour
1/8 teaspoon salt
Food coloring (optional)
Items to use for filling and decorating (e.g., chocolate pieces, peanut butter chips, nuts, maraschino cherries, white chocolate chips, or butterscotch chips.)

Icing
1 cup confectioner's sugar
3 1/2 tablespoons milk
1 teaspoon vanilla extract
Food coloring (optional)

Directions: Heat oven to 350°. Thoroughly mix together margarine, vanilla, sugar, and three drops of food coloring (any color) with a mixer on low speed for two minutes. Add flour and salt, and work until dough holds together. Mold dough by tablespoonfuls around a few chocolate pieces, nuts, or cherries. Place dough balls on a baking sheet approximately 1 inch apart. Bake for 10 minutes or until light brown.

Once the cookies are cool, dip tops into icing. Decorate with colored sugar, sprinkles, candies, or coconut. Yields 25 cookies.

Why the Traffic Jam Cookies

2 1/2 cups all-purpose flour
1/2 teaspoon baking powder
1 cup margarine or butter, softened
1 egg
1 cup sugar
2 teaspoons vanilla extract
1 cup jam, any flavor

Directions: Preheat the oven to 300°. In a bowl, combine flour and baking powder. Mix well and set aside. Next, in a medium-sized bowl, cream butter/margarine, sugar, egg, and vanilla extract. Beat at medium speed with an electric mixer until smooth. Add the flour mixture, and blend on low speed until combined. Roll the dough into 1-inch balls and place on a baking sheet, approximately 1 inch apart. With your thumb, press down the center of the dough balls to form a hollow in the middle of each ball; fill this with a small amount of jam (about 1/2 teaspoon). Bake 20 minutes or until golden brown. Makes 4 dozen cookies

Red Velvet Cupcakes. Photo and baking credit, Gina Meyers.

Red Velvet Cake

4 tablespoons cocoa powder
1 ounce liquid red food coloring
3/4 cup water
1 yellow cake mix, with pudding in the mix
4 eggs
1 teaspoon vanilla extract
1 teaspoon butter
4 tablespoons buttermilk
1 tablespoon white vinegar

Directions: Preheat oven to 325°. In a large bowl, mix cocoa powder, red food coloring, and part of the water to form a paste. Next, add all of the other ingredients except the white vinegar. Blend for 2 1/2 to 3 minutes with a mixer on medium speed. Then add the vinegar and mix with a spatula. Pour the batter into a bunt or round cake pan, and bake for approximately 35 minutes. This recipe can be made into cupcakes as well.

Adorn each cupcake or the entire Red Velvet Cake with various miniature die-cast Cullen cars, such as Carlisle's Mercedes S55 AMG, Rosalie's red BMW M3, Edward's silver Volvo S60R, Alice's yellow Porsche 911 Turbo, or Emmett's Jeep Wrangler. A replica of Bella's red Chevy pickup truck could also be added.

Jasper Cookie Bars

1/2 cup margarine or butter
1 1/2 cups graham cracker crumbs
1 (14-ounce) can sweetened condensed milk
1 (6-ounce) package semisweet or milk chocolate chips
1 (6-ounce) package of butterscotch or peanut butter chips
1 1/3 cup coconut flakes
1 cup chopped walnuts

Directions: Preheat the oven to 350°. Melt butter in a microwavable bowl, and add graham cracker crumbs to the melted butter. Place graham cracker crumb mixture in a 13- by 9-inch baking pan and press down with a fork, covering the bottom of the pan. Pour a can of sweetened condensed milk on top of graham cracker crumb mixture and then sprinkle with the remaining ingredients. Bake for 25 minutes. Once cooled, cut into bite-size squares.

Tip: Peanut butter chips, butterscotch chips, or white chocolate chips may be added to the recipe if desired.

Forbidden Love Coconut Lemon Crumb Squares

(Sinfully delicious!)
1 3/4 cups graham cracker crumbs
1/2 cup granulated sugar
3/4 cup all-purpose flour
1/2 cup coconut
3/4 cup margarine, melted

Filling
1/2 cup of granulated sugar
1 egg
1 cup fresh lemon juice, plus 1/4 teaspoon of lemon rind
1/2 cup of coconut flakes

Directions: Combine first four ingredients in a large bowl. Melt margarine and pour over graham cracker mixture, and work together until crumbly. Press the mixture into an ungreased 9- by 9-inch pan and set aside. Next, place filling ingredients in a pot over low heat, stirring until thickened for about four minutes. Pour filling over bottom layer. Cook for 25 minutes in a 350° oven. Makes approximately 30 squares.

Perfect for the Prom Bella's Bonbons

1/4 cup melted butter
1 can (14 ounces) of sweetened condensed milk
1 pound powdered sugar
1 package (14 ounce bag) coconut
1 package (11.5 ounces) chocolate chips
1/2 cube Parowax

Directions: Combine butter, milk, sugar, and coconut, and chill at least 30 minutes. Form into small balls and chill again. In a double boiler or a bowl placed over a pan of hot water, melt chocolate chips and wax. Dip balls into chocolate mixture quickly and remove with fork. Put on waxed paper to cool. Makes 2 dozen bonbons.

Sink Your Teeth into Peanut Butter Pie

(Don't forget the milk!)
1 (8-ounce) container frozen whipped topping
1 ready-made graham cracker crust
1/2 cup strawberry jelly
1 cup cold milk
1 package instant vanilla pudding mix
1/2 cup creamy peanut butter

Directions: Spread 1 cup of the whipped topping over the bottom of the crust. Drop jelly by the tablespoonful onto whipped topping. In a bowl, whisk milk and pudding mix together until thickened. Add peanut better and mix well. Then, fold in the leftover whipped topping; spread over the jelly. Allow to harden in the freezer for at least 2 hours. Serves 6 to 8.

Everyone enjoys different flavors … chocolate ice cream, strawberry, sorry about the food analogy.
—Bella speaking to her vampire boyfriend, Edward

Everyone Enjoys Different Flavors Sundae

Chocolate, vanilla, or strawberry ice cream
Hot fudge topping
Blanched slivered almonds (optional)
Fresh, seasonal berries (e.g., strawberries, blackberries, blueberries)
Maraschino cherries to top
Whipped cream

Directions: Heat fudge in either a saucepan or in the microwave (follow heating instructions on label). Spoon hot fudge onto scooped ice cream. Complete sundaes by adding fresh toppings, such as slivered almonds, berries, whipped cream, and cherries.

I like the night.
—Bella

Without the dark, we'd never see the stars.
—Bella

Starry Night Cake

1 1/4 cups all-purpose flour
1 cup granulated sugar
1 1/2 teaspoons baking powder
1/2 teaspoon salt
3/4 cup milk
1/3 cup shortening
1 egg
1 teaspoon vanilla extract
Star cookie cutter (or handmade star stencil)
Powdered sugar

Directions: Preheat oven to 350°. Grease and flour two 9-inch round cake pans. In a mixing bowl, add sugar, milk, shortening, egg, and vanilla extract. Blend the ingredients on medium speed for 2 minutes, slowly adding the flour, baking powder, and salt. Continue to blend for 3 more minutes, scraping the sides of the bowl with a spatula.

Once the cake batter is smooth, pour an equal amount of cake batter into each floured round pan. Bake 35 to 40 minutes on center rack and check for doneness by placing a toothpick in the center of the cake, if the toothpick comes out clean, the cake is ready. Once cake is cooled, place the star stencil on top. With a sifter, sift powdered sugar over the stencil, covering thoroughly. Gently remove stencil to reveal star shape. Repeat several times to create starry night.

It worked, your cooking skills have me soft as a marshmallow.-Bella

Twilight Chocolate Cake

2 1/4 cups all-purpose flour
1 2/3 cups granulated sugar
2/3 cup cocoa
1 1/4 teaspoons baking soda
1 teaspoon salt
1/4 teaspoon baking powder
1 1/4 cups water
3/4 cup shortening
2 eggs
1 teaspoon vanilla extract

Directions: Preheat oven to 350°. Grease and flour two 9-inch round cake pans. Place all ingredients into a large bowl and blend with an electric mixer on low speed for a minute. Increase to high speed and mix an additional 3 minutes, scraping the sides and bottom of bowl occasionally to make sure all of the ingredients have been mixed well. Pour the batter into the two greased and floured pans.
Bake for 30 to 35 minutes or until toothpick inserted in center comes out clean. Cool. Top with Midnight Frosting.

Midnight Frosting
1/2 cup sugar
1/4 cup corn syrup
2 tablespoons water
2 egg whites
1 teaspoon vanilla extract

Directions: Place sugar, syrup, and water in a saucepan. Cover the saucepan and boil over medium heat, mixture should boil in about four minutes. As the mixture boils, beat egg whites until stiff. Pour mixture from saucepan slowly into egg whites, beating constantly with electric mixer on medium speed. Add vanilla extract while beating.

I did once, on a dare
—Bella (ate dirt, that is)

Dare to Eat Dirt Pie

Foil cupcake liners
1 package of (10 ounce, pack of 24)Chocolate cookies, such as Oreos
4 pack prepackaged Chocolate pudding
Gummy worm candies

Directions: Crush cookies in a plastic bag until they are crumbs. Next, spoon chocolate pudding into a cupcake tin. Top chocolate pudding with cookie crumbs and then add gummy worms. Any variety of store-bought chocolate pudding will work, but I recommend using my Dare to Eat Mud Chocolate Pudding recipe.

Dare to Eat Mud Chocolate Pudding

1/3 cup sugar
2 tablespoons cornstarch
1/4 cup unsweetened cocoa powder
1/8 teaspoon salt
2 cups milk
2 egg yolks, slightly beaten
4 ounces of semisweet chocolate chips
2 tablespoons butter
2 teaspoons vanilla extract

Directions: Blend sugar, cornstarch, unsweetened cocoa powder, and salt in a 2-quart saucepan. Combine milk and egg yolks; gradually stir into sugar mixture. Slowly add the semisweet chocolate chips. Cook over medium heat, stirring constantly, until pudding thickens. Boil and stir 1 minute. Remove from heat, and stir in butter and vanilla. Serves 4.

Bella mentions Edward's eyes being the color of butterscotch.

Butterscotch Bars

1 cup all-purpose flour
6 tablespoons brown sugar
1/8 teaspoon salt
1/2 cup butter or margarine
6 ounce package butterscotch chips
1 tablespoon corn syrup
1 tablespoon water
2 tablespoons butter or margarine
1/8 teaspoon salt
2/3 cup walnuts, chopped (optional)

Directions: In a bowl, stir together flour, brown sugar, salt, and margarine or butter until crumbly. Press the mixture into an ungreased 9- by 9-inch pan. Bake in a 375° oven for 10 minutes. Next, combine the remaining five ingredients into a saucepan over low heat. Melt mixture and then add the walnuts, if desired. Pour the mixture over the first layer and place back into oven for 8 minutes. Once cooled, cut into squares. Makes approximately 25 bars.

Butterscotch Eyes

1 package (3.4 ounce) butterscotch instant pudding
2 cups applesauce
1/2 teaspoon ground cinnamon
1 cup thawed whipped topping (to be mixed into the pudding)
1 container of whipped topping, minus 1 cup (to be mixed into the pudding)
1 cup Teddy Grahams, honey variety

Directions: Mix dry pudding, applesauce, and cinnamon in medium bowl with a wire whisk for 2 minutes or until well blended. Gently stir in 1 cup whipped topping with the pudding mixture. Remaining whipped topping to be used in layering the alternate butterscotch mixture and whipped topping in parfait glasses. Garnish edges with Teddy Grahams. Note: You may have left over whipping topping. Makes 4 servings.

Love at First Bite Cupcakes

24 chocolate cupcakes (baked according to package directions on cake mix)
24 Nutter Butter cookies
Chocolate frosting
Vanilla Frosting
Tube of chocolate, green, and red decorator's icing

Directions: Frost cupcakes with the chocolate frosting. Ice the entire Nutter Butter cookie with white frosting, and use decorator's icing to draw a vampire expression on each cookie. Place vampire cookie in the middle of the cupcake.

Vampire Cupcakes

1 package of chocolate cake mix
1 can of chocolate frosting
Cupcake liners
Tube of red decorator's icing
Plastic vampire teeth

Directions: Prepare cupcakes according to the directions on the cake mix. Once cooled, frost with chocolate frosting. Top with plastic vampire teeth, and use red decorator's icing to resemble blood dripping from teeth.

Vampire Bites

½ cup of red peanut M&M's candies
1 (16-ounce) package white chocolate chips
2 cups small pretzel twists

Directions: Line a cookie sheet with waxed paper. Heat white chocolate chips in microwave about one minute to melt. Pour melted chips onto waxed paper and spread with a spatula. Next, add red peanut M&M's and pretzel twists. Once cooled, break off into tiny pieces.

Chocolate-Peanut Butter Coated Apples

10 wooden ice cream sticks
10 medium sized apples such as Gala, Granny Smith, Red Delicious, stems removed
10 ounces, 1 package of Peanut Butter Chips
½ cup of vegetable oil
2/3 cup of powdered sugar
2/3 cup of Hershey's brand cocoa powder

Directions: Insert a wooden stick into each washed and dried apple where the stem has been removed. Cover a tray with waxed paper and place apples on the wax paper. In a microwave safe bowl, place the peanut butter chips and oil. Microwave on high for one minute or until chips are melted when stirred. Check every 15 seconds to ensure you are not accidentally burning peanut butter chips. In the same microwave safe bowl, stir together cocoa powder and powdered sugar into the melted peanut butter chips, stirring until smooth. Return to microwave for another minute. Dip apples in the mixture, twirl to remove excess coating. Allow to cool on the prepared tray. Place in the refrigerator for ½ hour to ensure proper cooling of coated apples.

Oh, she does smell good!
—Alice

I hope you are hungry.-Esme

She already ate.-Edward

Vampire Bite Bars

Graham crackers
1 cup brown sugar
1/2 cup butter
1/2 cup milk
1 1/3 cups graham cracker crumbs
1 cup chopped walnuts
1 cup coconut
1/4 cup dried cherries

Directions: Line a 9- by 9-inch pan with whole graham crackers. In a saucepan, combine sugar, butter, and milk. Bring to a boil; simmer for about 2 minutes. Next, add cracker crumbs, nuts, coconut, and cherries; mix well. Pour over the whole graham crackers and refrigerate overnight. May add vanilla icing to top before cutting and serving squares.

Rocky Road Brownies

1 3/4 cups granulated sugar
3/4 cup butter, softened
3 large eggs
2 teaspoons vanilla extract
4 squares unsweetened chocolate, melted and cooled
1/4 teaspoon of salt
1/2 cup cocoa powder
3/4 cup flour
12 marshmallows
1 cup finely chopped walnuts
1 cup milk chocolate chips

Directions: Heat oven to 350°. Grease and flour a 9- by 13-inch pan; set aside. With an electric mixer on medium speed, cream sugars and butter until fluffy; then add eggs, and mix an additional 1 to 2 minutes. Add in the chocolate, vanilla extract, cocoa, flour and salt. Once mixed, stir in the chocolate chips and walnuts. Place marshmallows in greased pan, and spoon batter over the marshmallows. Bake on the center rack for 25 minutes. Once cooled, cut into squares.

As we walked in, Emmett ambled through the kitchen door, seeming perfectly at ease. Nothing ever bothered Emmett.-Bella

Get Out the Forks Lemon Pie, photo credit, David Meyers.

Get Out the Forks Lemon Pie

1 ready-made graham cracker crust
1 (3-ounce) package lemon-flavored Jell-O
1 cup boiling water
1/2 block soft tofu
4 ounces light whipped topping
1 tablespoon fresh lemon juice
1 teaspoon lemon rind

Directions: Dissolve the Jell-O in boiling water and cool. Add the tofu and blend with an electric mixer. Fold in the whipped topping, and add the lemon juice and rind. Pour into graham cracker shell and refrigerate until set.

Tip: This is a good substitute for lemon meringue pie if you are watching the calories.

Bella picks up an apple and states her curiosity to Edward, turning the apple around in her hands and asking him, what would he do if someone dared him to eat food?

Apple Cider Cheese Fondue

4 cups shredded sharp cheddar cheese
1 1/2 tablespoons cornstarch
1 1/4 cup apple cider
1/4 teaspoon lemon juice
1/4 teaspoon salt
1/8 teaspoon cinnamon
1/8 teaspoon nutmeg

Directions: In a medium-sized saucepan, over medium heat, warm cider and lemon juice until simmering. Next, toss cheese and cornstarch together and, one handful at a time, place into the simmering apple cider mixture, stirring constantly. Stir in remaining spices. Cover and simmer over low heat until thickened. Transfer to a fondue pot to keep warm. Dip toasted bread, sliced cooked sausage, or apple slices in fondue.

Apple of My Eye Pie

5 to 6 golden delicious apples, peeled, cored, and thinly sliced
2 tablespoons lemon juice
1/3 cup applesauce
1/3 cup light brown sugar
1/3 cup granulated sugar
1 teaspoon cinnamon
3 (9-inch) ready-to-bake pie crusts
1 egg white, beaten
2 tablespoons sugar, large crystal

Directions: Preheat oven to 450°. Mix apples, lemon juice, applesauce, brown sugar, sugar, and cinnamon, and set aside. Grease muffin pan. Roll out dough 1/8 inch in thickness and cut twelve 4-inch circles and twelve 3-inch circles out of the dough. Place one 4-inch circle in each muffin cup and fill with apple mixture. Top each mini pie with a 3-inch circle and press edges together. Cut 4 slits in each pie top. Brush each pie with egg white, and sprinkle with sugar. Bake for 15 to 18 minutes or until golden brown. Let cool before removing from muffin pan. Makes 12 servings.

Apple Cider Spice

12 broken cinnamon sticks
1/4 cup whole cloves
1/4 cup allspice berries
1 teaspoon nutmeg
Grated rind of 2 oranges
2 lemons, thinly sliced (to be used in cider mixture during simmering)
2 oranges, thinly sliced (to be used in cider mixture)

Directions: Combine the ingredients; use one teaspoon of the mixture per mug of cider. To use, simmer cider with the spices also add sliced lemons and slices of oranges for 10 minutes; strain before serving.

Hot Mulled Apple Cider

1/2 cup brown sugar
1/4 teaspoon salt
2 quarts cider
1 teaspoon whole cloves
1 cinnamon stick

Directions: Combine brown sugar, salt, and cider. Add spices and slowly bring to a boil in a pot; simmer uncovered for about 20 minutes. Remove the spices and serve warm.

Chunky Applesauce

9 cups sliced apples such as Fuji, Gala, McIntosh, Melrose, Golden Delicious varieties.
1/2 cup apple cider
1 tablespoon lemon juice
1/2 cup sugar
1/8 teaspoon salt
1/2 teaspoon nutmeg
Cream (optional)
Cinnamon (optional)

Directions: Combine the apples, cider, and lemon juice in a 3-quart saucepan. Bring to a boil over medium heat, and simmer until apples are tender, about 15 to 20 minutes. Next, add sugar, salt, and nutmeg, and cook for a minute or so longer. Stir apples to separate them into chunks. Top with cream and cinnamon to serve, if desired.

Tip: Be careful in choosing the variety of apple when making applesauce. Some varieties tend to become watery when cooked. Some of the best apples for making applesauce include Fuji, Gala, McIntosh, Melrose, Jonathan, and Golden Delicious.

Fried Apples

6 apples
1/4 cup butter or margarine
3 tablespoons of brown sugar

Directions: Quarter and core the apples, but do not peel. Melt the ¼ cup of butter in a frying pan on low heat and add the apples. Sprinkle with brown sugar, and cook slowly with a little bit of water until they are tender.

Apple Bread

3/4 cup vegetable oil
1 cup brown sugar
2 eggs
1 1/2 cups chopped apple
1/4 cup chopped walnuts
1 tablespoon lemon zest
1 1/2 cups flour
1 teaspoon cinnamon
1/2 teaspoon nutmeg
1 teaspoon baking soda
1/4 teaspoon salt

Directions: Mix all ingredients together and pour into a greased loaf pan. Bake at 350° for 55 minutes or until toothpick inserted comes out clean.

Tip: There are many ways to grease a pan. One of the easiest ways is by using a cooking spray. Simply spray the cooking spray evenly around the pan surface. Another way is to place vegetable shortening on a folded paper towel and apply the grease to the pan.

I Dare You American Apple Crisp

5 medium apples (Pippin or Granny Smith variety), sliced thin
1/2 cup yellow cake mix
½ cup sugar and cinnamon combination, ¼ cup of each
1/4 cup melted butter

Directions: Place sliced apples in a glass baking dish, and sprinkle with cake mix and cinnamon-sugar mixture. Pour melted margarine over the mixture. Bake for 25 minutes at 400°.

An apple a day hopefully won't keep Edward away.

Blushing Bella Apples

2 red baking apples, such as Cortland, Empire, or Fuji variety
1/4 cup butter
2 tablespoons flour
1 teaspoon cinnamon
1/2 cup brown sugar
1/4 cup chopped pecans

Directions: Preheat the oven to 400° (reduce heat to 350° when ready to place apples in the oven). Core the apples and place them in a baking dish. Melt the butter and then stir in the flour, cinnamon, and brown sugar. Spoon the brown sugar mixture into the center of the cored apples. Sprinkle with chopped pecans (optional). Bake at 350° for 30 minutes or until tender.

Tip: The best baking apple has to have a good sweet-tart balance and their flesh won't break down as they cook. Ask your local grocer or at a farmer's market what varieties they carry that are good baking apples. Some great baking apples include Cortland, Empire, Fuji or Gala varieties.

Werewolf Chow photo credit, Gina Meyers

How comfortable they seemed to be with their fate, here in this happy kitchen, none of these werewolves wanted the same fate for their friend.-Bella

Werewolf Chow

9 cups rice cereal, such as Chex brand
1/4 cup butter or margarine
1 cup chocolate chips, semisweet, or a combination of 1/2 cup chocolate chips and 1/2 cup peanut butter chips
1/2 cup smooth peanut butter, not crunchy
1 teaspoon vanilla extract
1 1/2 cups powdered sugar

Directions: Place the cereal in a large zip-seal bag. Next, microwave the chocolate chips, peanut butter, and butter or margarine for about 1 minute. If the mixture hasn't melted, stir and place in microwave for another 20 to 30 seconds. Once melted, stir in the vanilla extract. Pour the chocolate chip–peanut butter mixture over the cereal; then add the powdered sugar and shake. Spread the mixture on waxed paper to cool.

Too Hot to Handle

8 quarts plain popped popcorn
1 cup butter or margarine
1/2 cup light corn syrup
1 package cinnamon candies

Directions: Place popcorn in a large bowl and set aside. In a saucepan, combine butter, corn syrup, and red hot candies; bring to a boil over medium heat, stirring constantly. Pour the mixture over the popcorn and mix thoroughly. Place popcorn mixture into a baking pan and bake at 250° for 50 minutes. Remove from the pan and spread out on waxed paper to cool.

Port Angeles Snack Attack

2 (7-inch) flour tortillas
2 tablespoons strawberry cream cheese
1/4 cup raisins
1/4 cup dried cranberries
1 cup finely chopped green apples
1 teaspoon each of sugar and cinnamon combined
2 tablespoons margarine

Directions: In a medium-sized bowl, combine apples, cranberries, raisins, and sugar-cinnamon mixture. Melt margarine in a skillet over medium heat and fry each tortilla till crisp. Place tortillas on a paper towel to take off excess margarine and to cool. Once cooled, spread with cream cheese, and top with apple mixture.

Sugar Cookies. Photo and baking credit, Gina Meyers.

Sugar Cookies

1 cup butter
1/4 cup milk
1 teaspoon vanilla
4 cups flour
2 eggs
1 1/2 cups granulated sugar
1 teaspoon baking soda

Directions: Cut butter into flour. Combine sugar, eggs, milk, and vanilla. Mix all ingredients together. Roll out the dough onto a floured surface ¼ inch in thickness. Cut with an apple cookie cutter. Place on a baking sheet. Bake at 350° for 8 to 10 minutes. Yields 3 dozen cookies.

Good Luck Chocolate Chip Cookies recipe and photo by,
Gina Meyers

Good Luck Chocolate Chip Cookies
2 ½ cups of flour
1 teaspoon of baking soda
1 teaspoon salt
1 cup (2 sticks) butter, softened
¾ cup of granulated sugar
¾ cup of brown sugar
1 teaspoon of vanilla extract
2 large eggs
1 tablespoon of milk
1 2/3 cup of semi sweet chocolate chips
1 cup chopped walnuts (optional)

Directions: Preheat oven to 350 degrees. Combine flour, baking soda, and salt in a small bowl. Beat butter, granulated sugar, brown sugar, vanilla extract and milk in a large mixing bowl until creamy with the electric mixer on medium speed for about two minutes. Add eggs, one at a time, beating well after each addition. On low speed, gradually mix in the flour mixture then stir in the chocolate chips. Drop by rounded tablespoon fulls onto an ungreased baking sheet. Bake for 12 minutes or until golden brown. Cool on a waxed paper or on a wire rack. Yields 4 dozen cookies.

Golden Oatmeal Cookies

1 cup (2 sticks) unsalted butter, room temperature
1/4 cup vegetable shortening
1 cup light brown sugar
3/4 cup granulated sugar
2 large eggs
1 teaspoon vanilla extract
2 1/2 cups rolled oats
2 cups all-purpose flour
1/2 teaspoon baking soda
1/2 teaspoon salt
1/2 teaspoon ground cinnamon
1 cup dried dates, chopped

Directions: Preheat oven to 375°. In a large bowl, beat the butter and shortening until smooth. Next, add the sugars, again beating mixture until smooth. Add the eggs, one at a time, as well as the vanilla and then put aside. In a separate bowl, mix all of the dry ingredients, including the cinnamon. Once the dry ingredients have been mixed, add to wet ingredients; mix until well combined. Stir in the dates. Drop the batter by rounded tablespoonfuls 1 1/2 inches apart on a cookie sheet. Bake for 12 to 14 minutes.

Bella Chow Biscotti

3/4 cup butter
1 cup Sugar
2 eggs
1 1/2 teaspoons vanilla extract
2 1/2 cups flour
2 teaspoons ground cinnamon
3/4 teaspoon baking powder
1/2 teaspoon salt
1 tablespoon of anise seed
¼ cup of Almond slices

Directions: In a large bowl, cream butter and sugar with an electric mixer, until light and fluffy, beating in the eggs one at a time. Next, add the vanilla extract. In a medium sized bowl, mix in the dry ingredients of flour, baking powder, salt and cinnamon. Alternatively, add dry ingredients to the butter mixture beginning and ending with the dry ingredients. Stir in almonds and anise seed. Cover the dough and place in the refrigerator to chill for 10 minutes. Once chilled, take dough out of the refrigerator and divide into two parts; roll into approximately 9-inch logs. Place the logs on a lightly greased cookie sheet and flatten slightly with hands. Bake in a 350° oven for 30 minutes. Take out of the oven and cool for five minutes. While dough is still warm, with a sharp long knife, cut the dough in 1/2- to 1-inch-thick diagonal pieces. On the same cookie sheet, turn diagonal pieces on their sides and bake for an additional 5 minutes at the same heat setting. Makes about 3 dozen cookies.

First Love Chocolate Mousse variation.
Photo and baking credit, Gina Meyers.

First Love Chocolate Mousse

8 ounces semisweet chocolate chips
2 tablespoons strong coffee
2 tablespoons orange extract
1 egg yolk
2 egg whites
A pinch of salt
2 tablespoons sugar
1/2 cup heavy cream (or 1/2 carton of cool whip)

Directions: Melt the chocolate, with coffee added, over low heat. Remove from heat and add first the orange extract and then the egg yolk, stirring till the mixture is smooth. In another bowl, beat the egg whites and salt; add the sugar and beat with an electric mixture until stiff peaks form. Lastly, whip the cream until it is stiff; fold into the egg whites. Fold egg white mixture into the chocolate mixture. Place in the refrigerator, and chill until ready to serve.

Chocolate and Apricot Torte

1/2 cup unsalted butter
1 cup semisweet chocolate chips
5 large eggs, separated
3/4 cup sugar
1 cup ground almonds
1/3 cup dried apricots, finely chopped
Dried apricots and fresh strawberries for garnish

Directions: Melt chocolate chips and butter together in the top of a double boiler and cool. Beat the egg yolks with the sugar until they become pale yellow. Mix the cooled chocolate mixture into the egg and sugar mixture, and blend in the ground nuts and chopped apricots. Next, beat the egg whites until stiff, and fold into the chocolate mixture. Place a pan of water on the bottom shelf of a preheated 375° oven. Line the inside of a 9-inch springform pan with aluminum foil and spray with cooking spray. Pour in the batter and bake for 45 to 50 minutes. Remove from the oven and cool in the pan for 15 minutes. Release the sides of the pan and carefully place onto a serving plate. Peel off the foil and allow to cool completely. To serve, dust with ground almonds or powdered sugar. Garnish with strawberry halves and apricots.

Tip: Placing a pan of water on the bottom shelf helps keep the torte moist.

Love at First Sip
(Nonalcoholic Beverages)

Love at First Sip Soda
1 box red Jell-O
2 liters red soda

Directions: Prepare the Jell-O according to the package directions. Chill overnight. Next, place the chilled red soda into a punch bowl and add cut-up pieces of Jell-O.

Coke Slushy
Slushy maker
Rock salt
Ice
2 liters of Coke

Directions: Follow the directions provided with the slushy maker. You could also try using a snow cone maker. Place ice in the snow cone maker; set maker to finely chopped ice and then add soda.

Sparkling honey lemonade in citrus salt rimmed glasses
1 cup freshly squeezed lemon juice
½ cup honey
6 cups of sparkling water, cold
Zest of 1 lemon
Coarse salt
Lemon or lime wedges
Ice

Directions: heat lemon juice and honey in a saucepan over low heat, stirring constantly until honey is completely blended with the juice. Chill until cold, then stir and pour into a large pitcher. Add cold water and stir. Mix lemon zest with salt in a small dish. Rub the rim of the glasses with a wedge of lemon or lime. Invert glass into the dish of salt and turn to coat rim. Add ice and lemonade. Serves 4-6.

As always, I was electrically aware of Edward sitting close enough to touch, as distant as if he were merely an invention of my imagination.
—Bella

Invention of My Imagination
3 ounces of orange juice
1 banana
3 ounces of 7Up or Sprite
Strawberry soda
Optional: ice

Directions: Combine orange juice, sliced banana, 7Up, and strawberry soda in a blender and add some ice. Makes one beverage.

Bella lost her appetite, so she only got a bottle of lemonade to drink for lunch.

Lemonade Slushy
3 ounces of freshly squeezed lemonade
3 ounces of 7Up or Sprite soda
Lime wedge to garnish
Optional: ice

Directions: Mix all ingredients in a blender on low speed for about one minute or until mixture appears slushy. Makes one Lemonade Slushy.

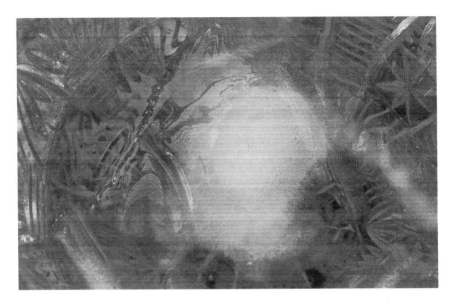

Blushing Bella. Photo credit, Gina Meyers.

Good luck tended to avoid me.-Bella

Blushing Bella
3 ounces of strawberry mango juice
3 ounces of freshly squeezed lemonade
Lime wedge to garnish

Directions: Mix all ingredients in a tall glass with ice and enjoy. Garnish with lime wedge on the side of the glass. Serves 1.

Bella Temple
Dash of grenadine
6 ounces of 7Up or Sprite
Cherry to top for garnish

Directions: In a glass, first add ice cubes. Next, add 6 ounces of 7 Up or Sprite, add a dash of grenadine, stir with a spoon and top with a maraschino cherry for garnish.

Werewolf Brew

3 cups apricot nectar
3 cups pineapple or orange juice
4 cups ginger ale or 7up
2 cups orange or lemon sherbet

Directions: In a large bowl, combine the apricot and pineapple juices. Just before serving, add the chilled ginger ale. Pour into glasses, and top with tiny scoops of sherbet.

Pomegranate Tea Recipe

3/4 cup instant tea
2/3 cup pomegranate juice
1/2 cup instant orange drink such as Tang
1 teaspoon ground allspice
1/2 teaspoon cloves

Directions: Combine ingredients and mix thoroughly. Stir in one tablespoon of mix per cup of water. Makes 1 3/4 cups of mix.

Vampire Venom Punch

1 (6-ounce) can frozen lemonade concentrate, thawed
1 (6-ounce) can frozen limeade concentrate, thawed
1 (20-ounce) can pineapple chunks, not drained
2 cups water
2 liters cherry soda, chilled
2 liters ginger ale, chilled
Lemon and lime slices

Directions: In a blender, mix concentrates with pineapple until smooth. Next, stir in water. Pour sodas into a punch bowl and add pineapple chunks. Garnish with lemon and lime slices.

You've given us an excuse to use the kitchen for the first time.-Carlisle

Vampire Blood Punch
1 (10-ounce) package frozen raspberries in syrup, thawed
4 cups pineapple juice
1 (6-ounce) can frozen lemonade concentrate, thawed
1 bottle (16- ounces) of 7Up
Ice cubes
Lemon or lime slices for garnish

Directions: In a punch bowl, combine thawed raspberries, lemonade concentrate, and the other ingredients. Garnish with lemon or lime slices, or both.

Pomme Punch, That's French for Apple
1 (14-ounce) can sweetened condensed milk
1 (46-ounce) can pineapple juice, chilled
1 (2-liter) bottle of strawberry soda, chilled
Raspberry sherbet

Directions: In a punch bowl, stir together sweetened condensed milk, pineapple juice, and strawberry soda. Top with sherbet, and serve over ice.

His fingers were ice-cold, like he'd been holding them
in a snowdrift before class.
—Bella

Ice-Cold Finger Punch
2 cans red punch concentrate
1 liter of 7Up or lemon-lime soda
2 latex gloves

Directions: Fill two clear plastic gloves with water, and tie off the ends
with a rubber band; place into the freezer. Once the hands are frozen,
about two hours. Once the clear plastic gloves and water is frozen, take
the "hand" out of the glove and discard the plastic glove and add the
hand to the punch bowl. In a punch bowl, mix 7Up with 2 cans of
red punch; add water according to the punch directions. You will have
floating hands that will also serve to keep the punch cold.

Cup of Charlie
Coffee maker
Paper filter for coffee maker (make sure it is the correct size for the
specific coffee maker)
French roast gourmet whole-bean coffee
Coffee grinder

Directions: In a coffee grinder, place the desired amount of beans for
brewing and grind. Next, place filter in the coffee maker and add freshly
ground coffee. Pour water into coffee maker (the more water, the weaker
the coffee will be). Turn on coffee maker and voila, in a few minutes you
have a cup of Charlie. Add sugar or creamer to coffee, if desired.

Edward's Thirst Quencher

3 large ripe peaches
3 large lemons
3 large oranges
1 cup sugar
3 cups strawberries
3 cups raspberries
1 (2-liter) bottle ginger ale, chilled
Ice cubes
15 to 20 strawberries

Directions: Peel and section the lemons and oranges, and remove the skins and pits from the peaches. Place the peaches, lemons, oranges, strawberries, raspberries, and sugar into a blender and blend until smooth. Pour into a punch bowl, and add ginger ale and ice cubes. Float strawberries and orange slices on top of Edward's Thirst Quencher.

Wolfbane On the Rocks Orange Julius

1/2 cup pulp-free orange juice
1/2 cup Sunny Delight
1 tablespoon vanilla extract
3/4 cup ice
1 tablespoon granulated sugar

Directions: Place all of the ingredients into a blender. Blend on medium speed until ice has been crushed and Julius is frothy. Add more ice and/or orange juice as needed.

Virgin Bloody Mary
1 (46-ounce) bottle chilled tomato juice
3 tablespoons horseradish
3 tablespoons freshly squeezed lemon juice
1 teaspoon Tabasco sauce
3/4 teaspoon Worcestershire sauce
Ice cubes
Lemon wedges (optional)
Celery (optional)

Directions: In a large pitcher, combine tomato juice, lemon juice, Tabasco, horseradish, and Worcestershire sauce. Stir until well blended. Fill 8 to 10 glasses with mixture, adding ice and a lemon wedge or celery stalk. Sprinkle with pepper, if desired.

> Just because I'm resisting the wine doesn't mean I can't appreciate the bouquet.-Edward

Twilight Tribute Punch
2 (10-ounce) packages frozen strawberries, defrosted
1 (6-ounce) can lemonade concentrate, thawed
1 quart ginger ale
2 cups raisins
6 gummy worms

Directions: Mix strawberries and lemonade concentrate in a blender until smooth. Add ginger ale and then transfer the beverage into a punch bowl. Stir in raisins. Drape gummy worms across the rim of the bowl.

Eclipse
1 cup black cherry soda
1 cup cranberry juice
1 cup ginger ale
Splash pineapple juice

Directions: Mix black cherry, cranberry juice, and ginger ale in pitcher. Add a splash of pineapple juice, and serve over ice.

New Moon Punch
1 gallon cranberry juice
1 gallon orange juice
1 cup raspberry sorbet
1 quart seltzer
Plastic vampire teeth

Directions: Mix the juices together. Add the sorbet and stir until it dissolves. Add the seltzer. May float plastic vampire teeth in punch bowl.

Howl at Twilight

(Cocktails)

Increments

1 cup	8 ounces
1 split	6.3 ounces
1 wineglass	4 ounces
1 pony	1 ounce
1 dash	1/32 ounce
1 jigger	1 1/2 ounces

Don't you want to know if I drink blood?
—Edward talking to Bella

Breathless
1/2 lime
1/2 ounce white crème de cacao
1/2 ounce Cointreau
1 ounce white Jamaica rum
Club Soda

Directions: Squeeze lime juice into a glass filled with ice cubes; save lime shell. Add to glass crème de cacao, Cointreau, and rum. Add club soda to fill glass. Stir. On the edge of the glass, decorate with a wedge of lime and fresh mint dusted with bar sugar.

Scotch and Water

Directions: Pour 1 to 1 1/2 ounces scotch over ice cubes in a 14-ounce highball glass. Serve a small pitcher of water alongside.

Bloody Mary
1 (46-ounce) bottle chilled tomato juice
3 tablespoons horseradish
3 tablespoons freshly squeezed lemon juice
1 teaspoon Tabasco sauce
3/4 teaspoon Worcestershire sauce
1 1/2 cups vodka
Ice cubes
Lemon wedges (optional)
Celery (optional)

Directions: In a large pitcher, combine tomato juice, lemon juice, Tabasco, horseradish, Worcestershire, and vodka. Stir until well blended. Fill 8 to 10 glasses with mixture, adding ice and a lemon wedge or celery stalk. Sprinkle with pepper, if desired.

Never Die
1/2 ounce rum
1/2 ounce dry vermouth
1/2 ounce gin
1/2 ounce sloe gin
1/2 ounce triple sec
1/2 ounce vodka
1/2 ounce whiskey
6 ounces of cola or fruit punch
Maraschino cherry
Pineapple or orange slice

Directions: In a cocktail shaker with ice, add the rum, dry vermouth, gin, sloe gin, triple sec, vodka, and whiskey and shake. Strain. Add cola or fruit punch to a tall glass and garnish with a pineapple, orange and maraschino cherry on a spear/cocktail stick.

Wicked Gin and Tonic
Fill glass with ice
1 shot Gin or Vodka
A twist of lemon or lime
1 can of chilled tonic water

Directions: Fill glass with ice. Add one shot of Gin, a twist of lemon or lime juice and fill remainder of glass with tonic water.

Gin and Tonic, photo by David Meyers.

Bad Vampire
1 part vodka
1 part Tia Maria

Directions: Stir with ice cubes. Strain into chilled cocktail glass.

Twilight Run Cocktail
1/2 ounce French vermouth
1/2 ounce Italian vermouth
1 ounce brandy
1/4 ounce Pernod
1/2 teaspoon Curacao

Directions: Stir well with ice cubes. Strain into 3-ounce cocktail glass.

Midnight Stroll Punch
1 quart brandy
1 quart sweet sherry
4 ounces maraschino liqueur
1/2 pint Curacao
4 quarts champagne
2 quarts club soda
Sliced fresh fruits
Halved seeded grapes

Directions: Prechill all liquid ingredients. Pour into a punch bowl, and add ice cubes and fruit. Serve punch in champagne glasses. Serves 35 to 40 people.

Bellaholm
1 ounce champagne
1 part orange juice
1 ounce of rum
1 ounce vodka
1 ounce Chambord, raspberry liquer
Lemon wedge

Directions: Cover rim of a chilled martini glass with sugar. Pour Chambord in glass. Mix vodka, rum and orange juice in a separate glass. Shake well with ice in a shaker. Pour contents of the shaker (vodka, rum, and orange juice) into the martini glass and add the Chambord. Top with champagne. Garnish with a lemon wedge. Serves 1.

Bellaholm, photo courtesy of David Meyers.

Forkshattan
1 1/2 ounces blended whiskey
1/2 ounce sweet vermouth

Directions: Place whiskey and sweet vermouth in a shaker with ice and then strain. For a dry Manhattan, use dry vermouth and garnish with a Greek olive on a toothpick.

Classic Cooler
1 bottle white wine
1 cup raspberries
1 liter Italian sparkling water

Directions: Mix all ingredients in a glass pitcher with plenty of ice and serve.

White Wine Mojito
1 bottle white wine
1 cup limeade juice
Fresh mint leaves
2 lime wedges

Directions: Mix all of the ingredients in a glass pitcher and place the lime wedges and mint leaves inside the pitcher.

Jasper Cocktail
1 ounce sweet sherry
1/2 ounce Italian vermouth
1 dash orange bitters

Directions: Shake with ice cubes. Strain into chilled cocktail glass.

Alice Cullen Cocktail
2 ounces Pernod
1/2 lump sugar

Directions: Half fill cocktail glass with shaved ice. Place sugar on top. Drip Pernod on sugar. Add a twist of lemon peel, and serve with cut straws.

Cafe de Amore
1 1/2 ounces gin
1 egg white
1 teaspoon Pernod or Herbsaint
1 teaspoon fresh cream

Directions: Shake well with ice cubes. Strain into chilled 4-ounce cocktail glasses.

Enchanted
1 ounce cognac
1/4 ounce green Chartreuse
1 teaspoon lemon juice
2 drops Angostura bitters

Directions: Shake with ice cubes. Strain into a chilled cocktail glass.

Cullen Cocktail
1 ounce Red Rum
3 ounces Coke or Pepsi
Lime as garnish

Directions: Fill a glass with ice cubes and Coke or Pepsi. Squeeze lime into the glass. Add rum, and stir.

Rum and Coke
1 ounce rum
3 ounces Coke or Pepsi

Directions: Add ice cubes to a glass. Next, add rum and Coke or Pepsi. Stir. If sugar content is of concern, you may use diet soda. For an added zing, use flavored colas, such as Vanilla or Cherry Coke.

Isabella Crown and Coke
1 ounce Crown Royal
3 ounces of Coke

Directions: Add ice cubes to a glass. Next, add the Coke and Crown Rum. Stir and serve.

Bella Italiano Cocktail
1 ounce absinthe
1/2 ounce anisette
3 dashed maraschino liqueur
1/4 ounce water

Directions: Shake with ice cubes. Strain into chilled cocktail glass.

Just a Dream
3/4 ounce evaporated milk
3/4 ounce white crème de cacao
3/4 ounce crème de noyaux

Directions: Mix ingredients and shake with ice cubes. Strain into a cocktail glass.

Shimmer
1 ounce Barbados rum
1 ounce Grand Marnier
1/2 ounce fresh cream

Directions: Shake with ice cubes. Strain into chilled cocktail glass.

White Cloud
3/4 ounce vodka
1/2 ounce white crème de cacao
1 dash evaporated milk
1 dash Lopez coconut cream

Directions: Shake with ice cubes. Strain into chilled cocktail glass.

Around the World
3 ounces orange juice
3 ounces lemon juice
3 ounces light Puerto Rican rum
1/2 ounce brandy
Juice of 1/2 fresh lime

Directions: Blend with 2 scoops of shaved ice for 12 to 15 seconds in an electric mixer. Pour into two large glasses. Fill glasses with cracked ice. Serve with straws. Makes 2 drinks.

Grandma Marie
1 1/2 ounces light Puerto Rican rum
2 ounces orange juice
Angostura bitters

Directions: Pour rum and orange juice over ice cubes in an old-fashioned style glass. Stir. Float a few drops of bitters on top.

Bella Brandy
1 ounce brandy
1 ounce crème de cacao
1 ounce heavy cream
1/2 cup ice

Directions: Combine all ingredients in a blender. Blend on medium speed for about a minute. Top with cocoa powder, cinnamon, or nutmeg, or a combination of the three.

Forks Cooler
Juice of 1/2 lemon
1/4 teaspoon sugar
2 ounces New England rum
Club soda

Directions: Shake lemon juice, sugar, and rum with ice cubes. Strain into a goblet. Add ice cubes. Fill with soda. Add a splash of rum on top.

Phil's Highball
2 ounces bourbon
Ginger ale

Directions: Pour bourbon over ice cubes in a highball glass. Fill with ginger ale. Add a twist of lemon peel. Stir.

Fast Pitch
2 ounces brandy
Ginger ale or club soda

Directions: Pour brandy over 1 ice cube in an 8-ounce highball glass. Fill with ginger ale or club soda. Add a twist of lemon peel. Stir gently.

Charlie Swan Sergeant Drink
4 ounces brandy
2 dashes Pernod
3 dashes Angostura bitters
1 teaspoon lemon juice
1 teaspoon sugar syrup
1 egg
Club soda

Directions: Shake all ingredients except soda with ice cubes. Strain into two tall highball glasses. Add ice cubes. Fill glass with soda. Dust with grated nutmeg.

Morning Glory Margaritas
(Makes 8 to 10 margaritas)
1 lime, cut into 8 to 10 wedges
8 to 10 toothpicks
8 to 10 maraschino cherries
1 pint tequila
1 cup orange liqueur, such as triple sec
1 cup freshly squeezed lime juice
Ice cubes
Rock (coarse) salt, to rim the margarita glasses

Directions: Place salt in a pie tin. Rub the rims of the margarita glasses with lime juice (may use lemon juice). Dip the rims of each glass into the salt. Next, place the tequila, orange liqueur, lime juice, and ice into a blender. Blend the mixture. On a toothpick, place cherry and small lime wedge. Pour mixture into the margarita glasses and garnish with lime and cherry. For a sweeter margarita, add 1 pint of fresh strawberries with the tequila, range liqueur, lime juice and ice. Make sure strawberries have been washed and stems removed prior to placing in the blender. Rim the margarita glass with sugar.

Love at First Sight Cocktail
1 1/2 ounces gin
4 dashes grenadine
Juice of 1/2 lime or lemon
1 egg white

Directions: Shake with ice cubes. Strain into a chilled double cocktail glass. Decorate with a mint leaf.

Moonlight
Juice of 1 lemon
1/2 tablespoon bar sugar
2 ounces calvados or applejack
Club soda

Directions: Shake lemon juice, sugar, and calvados with ice cubes. Strain into highball glass. Add 1 ice cube. Fill glass with soda. Decorate with sliced fresh fruit.

Once Bitten, Twice Shy
1/2 teaspoon grenadine
Club soda or ginger ale
2 ounces French vermouth
Spiral-cut lemon or orange peel

Directions: Stir grenadine and 2 ounces soda or ginger ale together in a 12-ounce glass. Fill glass with ice cubes. Add vermouth. Fill with soda or ginger ale, and stir again. Insert lemon or orange spiral, and dangle end over rim of glass.

Cullen Club Collins
1 ounce Chambord, raspberry liquer
2 ounces sweet and sour mix

Directions: Fill the glass with club soda and add ice., with a shot glass, pour the Chambord and add to the club soda and ice. May garnish with lime and a cherry.

Breaking Dawn Glory
2 ounces scotch or bourbon
2 dashes Pernod
1 egg white
1 teaspoon bar sugar
Juice of 1/2 lemon
Juice of 1/2 lime
Club soda

Directions: Shake all ingredients except soda with ice cubes. Strain into chilled large goblet. Fill glass with soda.

Holiday Eggnog
12 eggs, separated
2 cups bar sugar
1 teaspoon vanilla
1 1/2 gallons cold milk
1 pint brandy
1 cup Jamaica rum
Grated nutmeg

Directions: In a heavy-bottomed pot, lightly whisk the eggs and sugars and very low heat. Mix for three minutes or until mixture becomes thick and lemon colored. Keep heat on low, and slowly blend in the vanilla extract and milk. Stir in brandy and rum, pouring them into milk mixture very slowly. With clean beaters, beat egg whites until soft peaks form; gradually add remaining sugar, and beat until egg whites are stiff. Spoon egg whites over the top of the milk mixture, and sprinkle with nutmeg. Serve the eggnog warm. If you plan on drinking it cold, chill in the refrigerator for several hours. Serves 30 to 35 people.

> Your mood swings are kinda giving me whiplash.
> —Bella

Milky Way
1/2 ounce brandy
1/2 ounce Jamaica rum
1/2 ounce bourbon
6 ounces milk
3 drops vanilla

Directions: Shake well in commercial electric drink mixer with a large scoop of ice cubes. Pour into a 10-ounce glass. Add ice cubes to almost fill glass. Dust with grated nutmeg. Serve with a straw.

Arizona Comfort
Juice of 1/2 lemon
1/2 teaspoon bar sugar
2 ounces Southern Comfort
Club soda

Directions: Shake lemon juice, sugar, and Southern Comfort with ice cubes. Strain into a highball glass. Add 2 ice cubes. Fill glass with soda.

Baseball Cocktail
1 ounce gin
1/2 ounce French vermouth
2 dashes Angostura bitters

Directions: Stir with ice cubes. Strain into chilled cocktail glass. Add an olive.

Love at First Sip
1/2 ounce Benedictine
1 1/2 ounce bourbon

Directions: Stir with ice cubes. Strain into chilled cocktail glass. Add a twist of lemon peel.

Breaking Dawn
1/2 ounce lemon juice
1/2 ounce Cointreau
1/2 ounce white crème de cacao
1/2 ounce gin
1/2 ounce scotch or bourbon

Directions: Shake with ice cubes. Strain into chilled tiki stem champagne glass or other large saucer champagne glass.

Mai Tai
1 lime
1/2 ounce orange curacao
1/4 ounce rock candy syrup
1 ounce dark Jamaica rum
1 ounce Martinique rum

Directions: Cut lime in half; squeeze juice over shaved ice in a mai tai glass, saving one shell. Add remaining ingredients and enough shaved ice to fill glass. Hand shake. Decorate with spent lime shell and fresh mint.

Million Dollar Cocktail
2 teaspoons pineapple juice
1 teaspoon grenadine
1 egg white
3/4 ounce Italian vermouth
1 1/2 ounces gin

Directions: Shake well with ice cubes. Strain into chilled large cocktail glass.

139

Dry Martini
1 ounce gin
1/4 ounce French vermouth
1/2 teaspoon Pernod

Directions: Stir with ice cubes. Strain into chilled cocktail glass. Decorate with a pearl cocktail onion.

Little Red Chevy Truck
1 1/2 ounces vodka
Juice of 1/4 lime
7Up

Directions: Pour vodka and lime juice over ice cubes in an old-fashioned glass or glass mug. Fill glass with 7Up.

Lemon Drop
1 1/2 ounces plain or lemon vodka
3/4 ounce fresh lemon juice
1 teaspoon sugar

Directions: Place lemon vodka and freshly squeezed lemon juice into a shaker with plenty of ice. Add sugar and shake. Stain into a chilled cocktail glass. Can also line the rim of the glass with lemon juice and dip in sugar.

How you likin' the rain, girl?
—Mike Newton

Bone Shaker
2 ounces VooDoo Spiced Rum
1/2 ounce triple sec
1/2 ounce lime juice
3 ounces pineapple juice

Directions: Blend with crushed ice, and garnish with a lime wedge and a cherry.

Pucker Up Collins
1/2 ounce Sour Apple Pucker
1/2 ounce Peach Pucker
1/2 ounce Tropical Fruit Pucker
2 ounces sweet and sour mix

Directions: Fill a glass with ice. Next, add the Sour Apple Pucker, Peach Pucker, and Tropical Fruit Pucker, finish off the drink by adding 2 ounces of sweet and sour mix, stir and add a cherry for garnish. If you would like to cut down on the sweetness of the drink, pour some club soda into the drink.

When all the champagnes gone, improvise you know how Dr. Cullen loves his champagne! Just what the doctor ordered.

Dr. Cullen's Mock Mimosa
2 ounces of chilled London Dry Gin
2 ounces of chilled Orange Juice
2 ounces of chilled Tonic Water

Directions: In a high ball glass, mix all ingredients straight up, make sure all ingredients are cold. Over wise, may be served over ice.

Twilight Time for a Party Punch
6 ounces concentrated orange juice, thawed
1 ½ cups of pineapple juice
1 cup lemon juice
1 cup sugar
2 bottles champagne
1 bottle Chablis

Directions: Mix and keep cold. Just before serving, add 2 bottles of chilled champagne and 1 bottle of chilled Chablis.

You are my life now.
—Edward

Bella Loves Edward Punch
1/4 cup vodka
1/2 gallon raspberry sherbet
2 bottles pink champagne, chilled
2 cans 7Up, cold

Directions: In a punch bowl, mix vodka, 2 cans of chilled 7Up, sherbet and two bottles of pink champagne.

Substitutions

If you are out of	Substitute
Butter	Margarine or butter-flavored shortening
All-purpose flour	Unbleached flour or wheat flour
Dark brown sugar	Light brown sugar
Whole eggs	Brown eggs or liquid egg substitute
Oil	Applesauce
Chocolate	Carob
Olive oil	Vegetable or cooking spray oil
Lard	Shortening or butter
White rice	Brown
Nuts	Water chestnuts
Sour Cream	Nonfat plain yogurt

If you are out of	Substitute
1 tablespoon baking powder	1 teaspoon baking soda and 2 teaspoons cream of tartar
1 tablespoon cornstarch	2 tablespoons flour
1 cup milk	1/2 cup evaporated milk mixed with 1/2 cup water
1 cup buttermilk	1 cup regular milk plus 1 tablespoon vinegar or lemon juice
1 cup sugar	1 cup honey and then reduce other liquid ingredients in recipe by 1/4 of a cup

Weights and Measures

Equals	Same as
1 cup cake flour	7/8 cup of all-purpose flour
1 pound brown sugar	2 1/2 cups packed brown sugar
1 cup milk	½ cup evaporated milk with ½ cup water
1 pound powdered sugar	3 1/2 cups powdered sugar
1 tablespoon flour	½ tablespoon cornstarch
1 whole egg	2 egg yolks
8 to 10 egg whites	1 cup egg whites
A dash equals	Slightly less than 1/8 teaspoon
3 teaspoons	1 tablespoon
2 tablespoons	1/8 cup or 1 ounce
4 tablespoons	1/4 cup or 2 ounces
5 1/3 tablespoons	1/3 cup
8 tablespoons	1/2 cup
10 2/3 tablespoons	2/3 cup
12 tablespoons	3/4 cup
14 tablespoons	7/8 cup
16 tablespoons	1 cup or 1/2 pint or 8 ounces
2 cups	1 pint
2 pints	1 quart
2 cups	16 ounces
1/2 fluid ounce	15 milliliters
2 fluid ounces	60 milliliters
8 fluid ounces	240 milliliters
16 fluid ounces	480 milliliters
1/8 cup	30 grams
1/4 cup	60 grams
1 cup	240 grams
1 pound	480 grams

Herbs and Spices and their definitions

Basil	Sweet warm flavor with an aromatic odor. Good with lamb, fish, roast.
Bay Leaves	A pungent flavor, good in vegetable dishes.
Caraway	Has a spicy smell. Use in cakes, breads, soups.
Chives	Sweet mild flavor of onion. Herb is great in salads, potatoes, fish, and soups.
Curry Powder	A number of combined spices to give it a distinct flavor to such dishes as meat, poultry, fish, and vegetables.
Dill	Both the leaves and seeds are flavorful. Leaves can be used as a garnish or to spice dill pickles.
Fennel	Both seeds and leaves are used. Has a sweet hot flavor. Use in small quantities in pies and baked goods.
Ginger	A pungent root, this aromatic spice is sold fresh, dried, or ground. Used in preserves, pickles, cakes, cookies, soup, and meat dishes.
Marjoram	May be used both dry or green. Used to flavor fish, poultry, omelets, lamb, stew, and tomato juice.
Mint	Leaves are aromatic with a cool flavor. Excellent in beverages, fish, cheese, fruit desserts.
Oregano	Strong aromatic odor, use whole or ground to spice tomato juice, fish, pizza, omelets, chili.
Paprika	A bright red pepper, this spice is used as a garnish for potatoes, eggs and can spice up meat and soups.
Parsley	Used as a garnish when fresh or a seasoning. Can be used in fish, omelets, stuffing, and mixed greens.
Rosemary	Very aromatic, used fresh or dried. Season fish, stuffing, beef. Lamb, onions, eggs, and bread.
Saffron	Orange yellow in color, used as a flavor or to color foods. Used in soups, chicken and rice dishes mainly.
Sage	Use fresh or dried. Sage flowers are used in salads. May be used in fondue, beef, tomato juice, fish, and cheese spreads.
Tarragon	Leaves are hot and pungent. Used to flavor sauces, salads, meat, tomatoes, and dressings.

145

Cooking Terms

Braise To brown whatever one is preparing and to cook and cover it in its own fat, using the liquids to preserve the juices.

Caramelize To melt sugar slowly until it becomes brown and sticky.

Flambe To pour warmed liqueur or brandy over food, as with cherries jubilee, and then light on fire.

Julienne To cut into matchlike sticks, as with carrots or celery.

Marinate To let stand in a seasoned liquid for flavor or tenderness. The marinade can be placed in a large plastic bag or poured over the food item to be marinated.

Knead To work a mixture with your hands.

Scald To heat milk until tiny bubbles appear.

Twilight **Movie Cast**

Kristen Stewart	Bella Swan
Robert Pattison	Edward Cullen
Billy Burke	Charlie Swan
Ashley Green	Alice Cullen
Nikki Reed	Rosalie Hale
Jackson Rathbone	Jasper Hale
Kellan Lutz	Emmett Cullen
Peter Facinelli	Dr. Carlisle Cullen
Cam Gigandet	James
Taylor Lautner	Jacob Black
Anna Kendrick	Jessica Stanley
Michael Welch	Mike Newton
Christian Serratos	Angela Weber
Gil Birmingham	Billy Black
Elizabeth Reaser	Esme Cullen

New Moon **Movie Cast**

Kristen Stewart	Bella Swan
Robert Pattison	Edward Cullen
Taylor Lautner	Jacob Black
Billy Burke	Charlie Swan
Ashley Green	Alice Cullen
Nikki Reed	Rosalie Hale
Jackson Rathbone	Jasper Hale
Kellan Lutz	Emmett Cullen
Peter Facinelli	Dr. Carlisle Cullen
Cam Gigandet	James
Anna Kendrick	Jessica Stanley
Michael Welch	Mike Newton
Christian Serratos	Angela Weber
Gil Birmingham	Billy Black
Elizabeth Reaser	Esme Cullen
Rachelle Lefevre	Victoria
Justin Chon	Eric
Christina Jastrzembska	Gran
Dakota Fanning	Jane
Michael Sheen	Aro
Russell Roberts	Mr. Berty
Jamie Campbell Bower	Caius
Christopher Heyerdahl	Marcus
Curtis Caravaggio	Rogue Vampire
Daniel Cudmore	Felix
Charlie Bewley	Demetri
Chaske Spencer	Sam Uley

Graham Greene	Harry Clearwater
Adrien Dorval	Bob Marks, neighbor
Michael Adamthwaite	Chet
Giovanna Yannotti	Native American (not credited)
Hugo Steele	Biker (not credited)
Brenna Roth	Indian (not credited)
Justin Shenkarow	Voice
Cameron Bright	Alec
Justine Wachsberger	Gianna
Alessandro Federico	Police officer
Roberto Marchetti	Italian father
Maria Grazia Pompei	Italian mother
Tinsel Korey	Emily
Corinna Russo	Italian child
Edi Gathegi	Laurent
Alex Meraz	Paul
Bronson Pelletier	Jared
Kiowa Gordon	Embry Call
Tyson Houseman	Quil Ateara
Alexander Mendeluk	Fraternity boy #1
Hunter Jackson	Fraternity boy #2
Gavin Bristol	Fraternity boy #3
Sean McGrath	Fraternity boy #4

Eclipse Movie Cast
Theatrical Release day: June 30, 2010

Kristen Stewart	Bella Swan
Robert Pattison	Edward Cullen
Taylor Lautner	Jacob Black
Billy Burke	Charlie Swan
Ashley Green	Alice Cullen
Nikki Reed	Rosalie Hale
Jackson Rathbone	Jasper Hale
Kellan Lutz	Emmett Cullen
Bryce Dallas Howard	Victoria
Peter Facinelli	Dr. Carlisle Cullen
Elizabeth Reaser	Esme Cullen
Gil Birmingham	Billy Black
Alex Meraz	Paul
Bronson Pelletier	Jared
Kiowa Gordon	Embry
Tyson Houseman	Quil Ateara
Tinsel Korey	Emily
Xavier Samuel	Riley
Chaske Spencer	Sam Uley
Cameron Bright	Alec
Charlie Bewley	Demetri
Daniel Cudmore	Felix
Dakota Fanning	Jane
Sarah Clarke	Renee Dwyer
Anna Kendrick	Jessica
Michael Welch	Mike Newton

Christian Serratos	Angela
Justin Chon	Eric
Catalina Sandino Moreno	Maria
Jack Huston	Royce King
Julia Jones	Leah Clearwater
Booboo Stewart	Seth Clearwater
Jodelle Ferland	Bree

Twilight **Party Planning Guide**

Pick a scene from the *Twilight* movie. Choose your favorite moment: the baseball scene, perhaps the prom scene, maybe Bella meeting the Cullens for the first time. Perhaps, host your own *Twilight* movie awards night: dress up in fine evening wear and have your friends make their picks with your preprinted ballot. Decorate doorways, the birthday room, the front door, the kitchen, even outside if your party will be outdoors. Decorate with streamers, *Twilight* posters, and colorful balloons. You could personalize your event by baking your own cake from a recipe found in *Love at First Bite*, or you could order a specialty theme cake or seek ideas from Web sites on how to create your own original memorable cake.

Twilight inspired decorations, black tablecloth, red placemats, red cloth napkins, red plate, red mug, red flowers, apple scented candles, white twinkling lights, apple topiary perched atop a covered box with an additional black tablecloth draped over the box and red cellophane accents. Twilight book, Edward doll and apple.

A New Moon Celebration with an out of this world theme suitable for preteens or space lovers can consist of an Astronaut helmet for the centerpiece, black tablecloth, white plates, white mugs, apple, red candle with black candle holder, white lights, bubbles, celestial blowers, a black tablecloth, a rocket ship with the moon in the background invitation, a celestial favor box with an alien parachute toy, a dog stuffed animal, and glittery model magic fusion clay (such as glow in the dark, black stars or silver glitter compounds, as shown on the right).

Red, black, and white themed table. White plates with white cup and saucer, red cloth napkin tied up with a red bow, crystal champagne glass, crystal candy dish, red apple scented candle on a black pedestal, red flowers, black tablecloth, apple topiary in background, silver bulbs, a clear vase full of red apples, twinkling lights and red cellophane strips, and Twilight book.

A *New Moon* backpack with Jacob keychain, rugged hiking boots, a white plate with Shamrock shaped sugar cookies.

Bella's birthday party table setting as described in the New Moon book. Crystal champagne and water flutes, fine china with gold (or silver) rim, white tapered candlesticks, large pewter decorations with white finials, pink roses in vase, silk pink petals, faux pink roses arrangement and pink champagne truffles. A miniature die cast of the famous Pink lady (The Blue Boy, 1770 painting) from Thomas Gainsborough reminiscent of Bella.

Twilight Party Checklist
Cards
Invitations (e-cards or regular card invitations)
Gift wrap (solid black or red wrapping paper)
Thank-you notes
Colored ribbon to go with the theme
Tape
Name tags

Decorations

Streamers

Cups, utensils (just forks might be a cute idea), and plates

Hats (baseball caps if you are choosing the baseball scene for your party)

Balloons and a helium tank

Mylar balloons (apple shaped)

Centerpieces (such as a bowl of apples)

Noisemakers

Confetti

Napkins

Party favors

Banners and wall decorations

Activities
Twilight DVD
Twilight music and "Clare de Lune"
Games
Piñata
Craft paper
Crayons, paints, markers

Food
Drinks
Snacks
Cake and goodies
Main course
Camera and batteries

Twilight Saga Party Favor Ideas
Chocolate candy
Apple lollipops
Chocolate Chess pieces
Sparkling body powder
Movie posters
Tee-shirts
Collectible Cards
Unofficial Twilight Trivia book
Love at First Bite, The Unofficial Twilight Cookbook
Candy bars with special Twilight covers
Box of bandaids

Scavenger Hunt Items to hide Ideas
Baseball cap
Biology book
Romeo and Juliet book
A map of Arizona
A map of Washington
A fork
Plastic fangs

Countdown to Your *Twilight* Party

4 weeks before party
Select the day, time, and location
Choose the specific scene for your *Twilight* theme
Make a guest list (gather e-mail addresses)
Schedule a bounce house (if desiring one)

2 to 3 weeks before party
Send out invitations
Plan for the activities, decorations, and food

1 week before party
Shop for decorations, favors, supplies, and presents
Purchase a helium tank, order cake
If making a piñata, start now

3 to 5 days before party
E-mail friends to get a head count
Confirm location, and pay any deposits
Fill piñata with candy, packaged fruit snacks, or mini presents

2 Days before party
Decorate party areas

Day of party
Prepare punch and food
Pick up cake or finish decorating cake
Pick up Mylar balloons or fill your own balloons

Bella's Prom Planner

Things to Consider

Plan your prom budget

Search online and through fashion magazines for form-flattering styles, latest news, and newest fashions.

Decide who you are going with. Do you feel comfortable asking the love of your life, Edward, or will you be taking a friend, such as Jacob?

Start making arrangements for hair, nail, and makeup appointments.

Take your girlfriends out to the mall to pick matching accessories, such as shoes, jewelry, purse, and, if it is anticipated that it will be cold, perhaps a shawl (or maybe Edward will let you wear his coat).

If you will be renting a vehicle, decide what kind and how large. If it is a limousine, see if friends will be pitching in. You know how fast Edward drives and how cute his car is, so maybe not a limo this time.

Purchase the prom dress.

Order Edward or Jacob's boutonnière.

Remind Edward or Jacob what color you'll be wearing, so he can choose the right color and style of corsage.

Four months before the prom

It is never too early to start looking for a dress.

Three months before the prom

Brainstorm who is available and who you'd like to take as your date, or maybe who you'd like to ask you.

The prom is expensive, so create a budget. Maybe start asking your boss for a few extra hours, or do a few extra chores around the house to see if your parents will chip in.

Sign up for an etiquette class, or brush up on your manners by reading a book. Check local churches to see if any are putting on fashion shows or conducting manners classes.

Look in magazines and clip out pictures of different hairstyles. There are even online programs that allow you to upload your photo and try on different hairstyles without going to the hairdresser and making it permanent.

Two months before the prom

Go on an out-of-town trip to the garment district and try factory outlet dresses. San Francisco, for instance, has a Gunne Sax outlet, with merchandise reduced by as much as 75 percent off retail. If you can't find anything that you love, consider patronizing the local bridal boutique in your area. If all else fails, order a dress online (but first get your measurements taken at a bridal, prom outlet, or local fabric store).

Check out the tux shop with your date. If you want his cummerbund to match your dress, you might want to bring a swatch of the dress to the tux shop.

Make your hair, manicure, pedicure appointments. If you are getting your makeup done professionally, start checking out the different makeup companies that offer assistance with makeup application. Find out if they charge a flat rate or if you need to purchase the products.

Work on obtaining your accessories, such as shoes, jewelry, and purse. Discuss your pre- and postprom plans. If your plans involve a limousine or a fancy restaurant, make sure your date has reserved both.

30 days before the prom

Have your dress professionally altered, if it needs alterations.

Start walking around the house in your shoes, so they aren't a shock on your feet the day of the prom. Purchase blister ointment if needed.

Order the boutonniere from your local floral shop. If your date is ordering your corsage from the same shop, maybe you can get a discount for ordering both from the same place. At the very least, you can make sure they match accordingly.

Two weeks before the prom

Purchase the prom bids.

Bella's prom day dos!

Pick up your date's boutonniere.

Prepare your purse with the essentials.

Make sure you or your date has possession of the prom bids.

If your school requires identification, make sure you and your date have proper identification.

If your school has certain rules, such as dress and hair codes, make sure your date is in compliance with those restrictions.

Have a wonderful time!

Prom Purse Essentials

Breath spray, Tic Tacs or mints

Money

Cell phone

Cell phone charger

Mini sewing kit

Bobby pins, mini hair spray

Prescription glasses or contacts, if needed

Safety pins

Powder

Shimmer blush

Mini perfume or perfume sample

Emergency mini deodorant

Extra panty hose

101 Random Bits and Pieces of the Twilight Saga

1. Vladimir and Stefan formed a coven in the City of Romania.
2. When Edward was human, his eyes were green colored and he was 6'2" in stature. The Volturi was formed by Marcus, Aius, and Aro, as well as their wives.
3. In the year 500 AD, there was a Volturi war and Romanian coven.
4. The Denali Coven happened sometime in the year 1000 AD.
5. Sasha transformed Kate, Tanya, and Irina.
6. The Volturi killed Sasha.
7. Carlisle Cullen was born in London, England.
8. Carmen and Eleazar, which were born in the 1700s, are part of the Denali Coven.
9. Carlisle became a vampire and later transformed Esme.
10. Civilized vampires in the early 1700s were discovered in Italy by Carlisle.
11. Jasper was born in Texas.
12. Jasper's original last name was Whitlock.
13. Jasper served in the Confederate Army while he was human.
14. Jasper Whitlock served in the American Civil War and became a major.
15. A woman named Maria changed Jasper into a vampire.
16. Esme Anne Platt was born in Columbus, Ohio, in the year 1895.
17. Bella's parents, Charlie and Renee, are divorced.
18. Edward Anthony Masen (Cullen) was born on June 20, 1901.
19. Edward's human parents were Edward and Elizabeth Masen.
20. Edward was born in Chicago, Illinois.
21. Isabella Swan was born to Charlie and Renee Swan on September 13, 1987.
22. Stephenie Meyer had a brilliant dream about an average girl and a sparkly, beautiful vampire. The dream became the manuscript *Twilight*.
23. Stephenie Meyer initially named her book *Forks*.
24. Edward Cullen is a vampire.
25. Jacob Black is a werewolf.

26. Werewolves and vampires do not get along.
27. The Cullens are a more evolved vampire; they do not suck human blood.
28. Members of the Cullen family consider themselves "vegetarian vampires."
29. The exact date that Stephenie Meyer began to write *Twilight* was June 2, 2003.
30. Stephenie Meyer resides in the Arizona area with her husband and three boys.
31. After Stephenie Meyer had the dream about vampire and human love, she had to take her children to their first day of swimming lessons.
32. Mary Alice Brandon Cullen was born in Biloxi, Mississippi.
33. In the early 1900's, Carlisle moved to Columbus, Ohio, to practice medicine.
34. Carlisle met a teenage Esme in the hospital in the year 1911. They later became a vampire couple.
35. When Carlisle and Esme first met, Esme was sixteen years old.
36. The name Esme is a derivative of the French word Aimee, which means "beloved."
37. The name Edward means "happy protector."
38. The name Isabella is a favorite name of Stephenie Meyers.
39. A nickname for Isabella is Bella or Bells.
40. The name Isabella means "consecrated to God."
41. Edward and Bella fall madly in love.
42. Edward and Bella eventually marry and have a child.
43. The story *Twilight* takes place mainly in Forks, Washington.
44. Forks, Washington, is one of the rainiest places in the United States.
45. Stephenie Meyer consulted with the Google search engine to find the rainiest place in the United States.
46. After the amazing success of *Twilight*, Stephenie Meyer visited Forks.
47. Edward Cullen considers himself a monster.
48. Many of the vampires in *Twilight* have special powers.
49. Bella moved to Forks, Washington, to live with her father while her mother traveled with her stepfather Phil and his baseball team.

50. Bella had only spent summers in Forks, Washington, prior to moving there for the school year of her sixteenth year.
51. Sam Uley is the leader of the werewolves.
52. Jacob Black is in love with Bella Swan.
53. Edward Cullen is concerned about his soul.
54. Bella Swan wants to be a vampire from the time she and Edward meet.
55. Bella eventually becomes a vampire.
56. Edward, in *New Moon*, thinks Bella has died, so he goes to Italy to have the Volturi take his life.
57. The Volturi deny Edward's request to die, and he and Bella are reunited.
58. Bella Swan is Italian.
59. Bella is accident prone.
60. Bella feels at home in Forks because of her pale skin and shy disposition.
61. Edward's skin is shimmery.
62. Vampires never age.
63. Bella attends Forks High School.
64. Forks High School's mascot is the Spartans.
65. Rosalie Lillian Hale was born in Rochester, New York.
66. Of the Cullen clan, Rosalie is the most upset over being a vampire.
67. Emmett McCarty was born in Tennessee.
68. In her human life, Esme married Charles Evenson, who went off to fight in World War I.
69. The great flu epidemic took the life of Edward's parents on or around 1917.
70. Edward was transformed into a vampire by Carlisle.
71. Carlisle works as a physician and has the rare ability not to be tempted by human blood.
72. Edward Cullen is ravenous over Bella's scent.
73. It is believed that Alice was changed into a vampire by an individual who worked at a mental institution.
74. Esme became pregnant by her husband, Charles Evenson, and moved to Ashland. There she tried to commit suicide after she lost her baby. Carlisle was working as a physician in Ashland at the time.

75. Close to the year 1921, Esme was transformed, as Carlisle saved her from impending mortality.

76. Carlisle and Esme became an item, fell in love, and married.

77. Alice and Jasper found one another in the 1940s and became companions.

78. Rosalie was abused by her fiancé and his friends.

79. Rosalie's fiancé left her for dead, but she was changed by Carlisle.

80. Rosalie found Emmett, who was attacked by a bear.

81. Carlisle transformed Emmett into a vampire.

82. In the 1930s, the Cullens moved to the Forks area due to its climate.

83. There is a treaty between the vampires and the werewolves.

84. Bella was born in Forks, Washington.

85. Renee left Charlie and took Bella to Riverside and then to Phoenix, Arizona.

86. The werewolves call the vampires "the cold ones."

87. The vampires do not eat or sleep, and cannot go out in the sun, for fear of being noticed, exposed.

88. Edward is a very fast runner.

89. Edward has the ability to hear people's thoughts but is unable to hear Bella's.

90. The meadow is a special place where Bella and Edward go.

91. To date, December 30, 2009, there are two books from the saga that have been made into movies: *Twilight* and *New Moon*.

92. Currently, *Eclipse* is being filmed.

93. *Eclipse* will premiere on June 30, 2010.

94. *New Moon*, to date, is the third-highest grossing movie of all time.

95. Edward takes Bella to an Italian restaurant in *Twilight*, where she orders Mushroom Ravioli.

96. Mike Newton, a classmate, invites Bella to a movie.

97. The name of the movie that they see is *Face Punch*.

98. "Life is short, and then you die."

99. Bella is transformed by her nineteenth birthday.

100. Bella thinks and talks a lot about age, since Edward will be seventeen forever.

True/False

Stephenie Meyer makes an appearance in the movie *New Moon*.
Answer: False, she appears as an extra in *Twilight*.

Rosalie and Jasper are a couple.
Answer: False, Jasper and Alice are a couple, and Emmet and Rosalie are a couple.

In *Twilight*, Bella borrows her prom dress from Alice.
Answer: True

La Push is the only beach that the Cullens are allowed on.
Answer: False

Esme is the mother of the Cullen children.
Answer: True

The three nomadic vampires that show up during the Cullen baseball game are named Lauren, James, and Victoria.
Answer: False, their names are Laurent, James, and Victoria.

Jasper and Rosalie are the two adopted Hales.
Answer: True

Carlisle and Esme adopted the two Hale twins.
Answer: True

Victoria creates all of the newborns in *Eclipse*.
Answer: True

There were about twenty newborns.
Answer: True

Jacob did violate the Quileute Treaty with the vampires by telling Bella that Edward is a vampire.
Answer: True

In *Twilight*, the first words that Jacob Black says to Bella are, "You are Isabella Swan, aren't you!"
Answer: True

Twilight won the Best Movie Award at the MTV Movie Awards.
Answer: True

Jacob Lautner did not win the People's Choice Award for Favorite Breakout Movie Actor.
Answer: False

Alice does not remember her past.
Answer: False, she does. It is just a little bit blurry.

Rosalie wishes she was human still.
Answer: True

Stephenie Meyer consulted her brothers, who are auto enthusiasts.
Answer: True

Edward never owned a Volkswagen Rabbit.
Answer: True

Easy *Twilight* Trivia

What is Bella's first name?
  A. Isabella
  B. Bellina
  C. Alexandra
Answer: Isabella

Name Bella's dad.
  A. Henry
  B. Ringo
  C. Charlie
Answer: Charlie

What is their last name?
  A. Duck
  B. Swan
  C. Goose
Answer: Swan

What does Bella's dad do for a living?
  A. He is a commercial fisherman
  B. He is a fireman
  C. He is a police chief
Answer: He is a police chief

Name the town Bella's dad resides?
  A. Seattle, Washington
  B. Forks, Washington
  C. Spoons, Nevada
Answer: Forks, Washington

Bella recently left what town to be closer to her dad?
  A. Phoenix, Arizona
  B. Dallas, Texas
  C. Tucson, Arizona
Answer: Phoenix, Arizona

Bella's dad lives in a:
   A. Small town
   B. Big city
   C. The suburbs
Answer: Small town

Edward is a cute guy, who happens to be what?
   A. A werewolf
   B. A vampire
   C. A zookeeper
Answer: A vampire

The Cullen clan call themselves what?
   A. Vegetarians
   B. Carnivores
   C. Typical Vampires, "I want to suck your blood."
Answer: Vegetarians

What Bible quote is found in *Twilight* in the beginning pages?
   A. But of the tree of the knowledge of good and evil, thou shalt not eat of it, for in the day that thou eatest thereof thou shall surely die. (Gen. 2:17)
   B. For God so loved the world that he gave his only son, that whosoever believes in him, will not perish but have everlasting life. (James 3:16)
   C. All we like sheep have gone astray, we have turned everyone to his own way, and the Lord has laid on him the iniquity of us all. (Isa. 53:6)
Answer: But of the tree of the knowledge of good and evil, thou shalt not eat of it, for in the day that thou eatest thereof thou shall surely die. (Gen. 2:17)

Despondent over Edward's apparent rejection, Bella escapes to the forest. Who finds her?
   A. Sam Uley
   B. Jacob Black
   C. Edward Cullen
Answer: Sam Uley

Name Bella's grandmother.
   A. Gina
   B. Marie
   C. Isabella
Answer: Marie

Name Bella's stepdad.
   A. Phil
   B. Charlie
   C. Sam
Answer: Phil

What color does Bella use to describe the color of Edward's eyes?
   A. Butterscotch
   B. Lemon yellow
   C. Peanut butter brown
Answer: A. Butterscotch

What do vampires do in the sun?
   A. Sparkle
   B. Turn blue
   C. Nothing
Answer: Sparkle or shimmer

What instrument does Edward play?
   A. Guitar
   B. Piano
   C. Nothing
Answer: Piano

When were the People's Choice Awards held?
   A. June 6, 2009
   B. January 6, 2010
   C. June 6, 2010
Answer: January 6, 2010

Planes, Trains, and *Twilight* Mobiles

Name the music that Bella hears in Edward's car.
   A. "Clair de Lune" by Debussy
   B. Spring Allegro by Vivaldi
   C. The Nutcracker Suite by Tchaikovsky
Answer: "Clair de Lune" by Debussy

Bella's car is a red
   A. Old Chevy truck
   B. BMW
   C. Toyota Tundra
Answer: Old Chevy truck

What is the make and color of Edward's car in *Twilight*?
   A. Silver Volvo
   B. Black Mercedes
   C. Silver Mercedes
Answer: Silver Volvo

What is the make, color, and year model of Bella's pickup truck?
   A. 1957 Chevrolet truck
   B. 1953 Chevrolet truck
   C. 1963 Ford truck
Answer: 1953 Chevrolet pickup truck

What color was Bella's pickup truck?
   A. Red
   B. Blue
   C. Rust
Answer: Red

Which type of motorcycle did Edward own?
   A. Ducati 848
   B. Honda
   C. None of the above
Answer: Ducati 848

Name the type of Mercedes owned by Bella.
  A. Guardian
  B. 300 Series
  C. Bella didn't own a Mercedes
Answer: Guardian

Which car from the list below did Bella own?
  A. Ferrari f430, colored blue
  B. Ferrari f430, colored red
  C. Ferrari f430, colored yellow
Answer: Ferrari f430, colored red

Fill in the blanks:
_____ owned a Volvo S60R, colored _____.
  A. Edward, silver
  B. Jacob, black
  C. Carlisle, black
Answer: Edward, silver

_____ owned an Aston Martin V12 Vanquish, colored _____.
  A. Carlisle, silver
  B. Edward, silver
  C. Alice, white
Answer: Edward, silver

What type of Volkswagen does Jacob own?
  A. Bunny
  B. Rabbit
  C. Station Wagon
Answer: Rabbit

What color is Jacob's Volkswagen?
  A. Blue
  B. Black
  C. White
Answer: Black

Place the motorcycle with the owner:
Ducati 848
  A. Edward
  B. Jacob
  C. Carlisle
Answer: Edward

Harley Davidson Sprint
  A. Charlie
  B. Jacob
  C. Edward
Answer: Jacob

Rosalie owned what make and color of vehicle?
  A. BMW, colored red
  B. BMW, colored blue
  C. Mercedes, colored black
Answer: BMW, colored red

Alice's car is a _____ 911 Turbo, colored _____.
  A. Porsche, yellow
  B. Porsche, blue
  C. Porsche, white
Answer: Porsche, yellow

What color is Emmett's Jeep Wrangler?
  A. Blue
  B. White
  C. Red
Answer: Red

What kind of vehicle does Rosalie drive, and what is its color?
  A. A red BMW M3 convertible
  B. A red Jeep Wrangler
  C. A red Porsche 911 Turbo
Answer: A red BMW M3 convertible

Who Said It?

"It would be more ... prudent for you not to be my friend. But, I'm tired of trying to stay away from you."
   A. Bella
   B. Edward
   C. Jacob
Answer: Edward

"Breakfast time, he said casually kidding and you said I couldn't act."
   A. Edward
   B. Charlie
   C. Jacob
Answer: Edward

"Breakfast for the human, milk and cereal."
   A. Phil
   B. Charlie
   C. Edward
Answer: Edward

"Last night I'd discovered Charlie couldn't cook much besides fried eggs and bacon."
   A. Alice
   B. Bella
   C. Jacob
Answer: Bella

Who does Bella say these words to: "It doesn't matter to me what you are!"
   A. Jacob
   B. Edward
   C. Alice
Answer: Edward

What does Alice say about Bella?
   A. "Oh, she does smell good!"
   B. "I can't wait to suck her blood."
   C. "She can see dead people."
Answer: A. "Oh, she does smell good."

Cullen Confidential

Name Edward's vampire sisters.
   A. Alice and Rosalie
   B. Renee and Bella
   C. Rosalie and Esme
Answer: Alice and Rosalie

Who is the last vampire to be killed?
   A. Esme
   B. Alice
   C. Victoria
Answer: Victoria

Name Edward's vampire brothers.
   A. Jacob and Charlie
   B. Jasper and Emmett
   C. Jacob and Jasper
Answer: Jasper and Emmett

In *Twilight*, who tries to kill Bella?
   A. No one, luckily
   B. A group of nomadic vampires, James, Laurent, and Victoria
   C. Jacob and the wolf pack
Answer: A group of nomadic vampires, James, Laurent, and Victoria

In their time of need, which clan rejects the Cullen family?
   A. Denali
   B. Cullen
   C. Maserati
Answer: Denali

What did the treaty between the Quileutes and the vampires state?
   A. That they both have there own separate land and that a vampire
       cannot change a human into a vampire
   B. That vampires and werewolves live together on the same land
   C. There is no treaty between the groups
Answer: That they both have there own separate land and that a vampire
cannot change a human into a vampire

Alice lived in what year and in what town before she became a vampire?
- A. San Francisco in 1957
- B. Mississippi in 1901
- C. France in 2001

Answer: Mississippi in 1901

What was the reason that Edward transformed Bella into a vampire?
- A. She was dying
- B. She desperately wanted to become a vampire, and he accommodated her
- C. Her never did turn Bella into a vampire

Answer: She was dying

Name the vampire that Edward dated from the Denali clan.
- A. Kate
- B. Makenna
- C. Tanya

Answer: Tanya

What is the game that the Cullens like to play during thunderstorms?
- A. Football
- B. Soccer
- C. Baseball

Answer: Baseball. Due to the strength of the Cullen family, they need a thunderstorm in order to cover up the sound of them hitting a baseball.

What kind of animal does Edward like to hunt?
- A. Fox
- B. Deer
- C. Mountain lions

Answer: Mountain lions

The Cullens lived where before Forks, Washington?
- A. England
- B. Rhode Island
- C. Alaska

Answer: Alaska

What did Emmett give Bella for her birthday?
  A. A new truck
  B. A new stereo for her truck
  C. Nothing
Answer: A new stereo for her truck

Name Edward's mom.
  A. Elizabeth Masen
  B. Renee Swan
  C. Alice Brady
Answer: Elizabeth Masen

What city was Edward born in?
  A. Bristol, England
  B. Chicago, Illinois
  C. London, England
Answer: Chicago, Illinois

When was Edward Masen Cullen born?
  A. June 1, 1901
  B. June 20, 1901
  C. July 20, 1901
Answer: June 20, 1901

What year was Edward transformed into a vampire?
  A. 1902
  B. 1989
  C. 1918
Answer: 1918

Edward Cullen retains the body of a?
  A. Ninety-year-old
  B. Sixteen-year-old
  C. Seventeen-year-old

Who transforms Edward into a vampire?
>   A. Esme Cullen
>   B. Carlisle Cullen
>   C. Elizabeth Masen

Answer: Carlisle Cullen

Why doesn't Rosalie like Bella?
>   A. She is jealous because she wishes she were human too
>   B. She isn't jealous because she likes being a vampire
>   C. Rosalie likes Bella

Answer: She is jealous because she wishes she were human too

The Dog Squad

Who is the alpha dog of Jacob's pack?
    A. Sam
    B. Jacob
    C. Paul
Answer: Sam

What is Jacob's normal body temperature?
    A. Too hot to handle
    B. 108°
    C. 96°
Answer: 108°

It was recently announced that Jacob Lautner will be the next star in what?
    A. *Northern Lights*
    B. *Twilight II*
    C. No announcement was made
Answer: *Northern Lights*

In *Twilight*, what does Bella prepare for her dad Charlie, Billy Black, and Jacob, Billy's son?
    A. Cheeseburgers
    B. Grilled cheese sandwiches
    C. Pasta
Answer: Grilled cheese sandwiches

Who does Jacob imprint upon?
    A. Bella
    B. Rosalie
    C. Renesmee
Answer: Renesmee

Sam Uley is the:
    A. Leader of the wolf pack
    B. A human that Bella goes to school with
    C. A vicious vampire
Answer: Leader of the wolf pack

Bella's Briefcase

Bella's bedding is what color?
    A. Red
    B. Blue
    C. Purple
Answer: Purple

What is the Forks High School nickname?
    A. Bears
    B. Spartans
    C. Eagles
Answer: Spartans

What sport does Bella's step dad play?
    A. Soccer
    B. Football
    C. Baseball
Answer: Baseball

When is Bella's birthday?
    A. October 13
    B. September 13
    C. November 11
Answer: September 13

How old was Bella when she spent her last Christmas in Forks, Washington?
    A. 4
    B. 3
    C. 2
Answer: 4

Who is James?
    A. A friend of Bella's
    B. A bad vampire tracker
    C. A werewolf
Answer: A bad vampire tracker

Where does James lure Bella?
  A. Her old ballet studio
  B. Her house in Forks
  C. To Forks, Washington
Answer: Her old ballet studio

What injuries does Bella sustain from James's attack?
  A. A broken leg, a crushed skull, broken ribs, blood loss, and bruises
  B. No injuries
  C. A vampire bite
Answer: A broken leg, a crushed skull, broken ribs, blood loss, and bruises

In *Twilight*, what is the Forks High School prom theme?
  A. Las Vegas
  B. Hawaiian
  C. Monte Carlo
Answer: Monte Carlo

What kind of food does Bella order at the Italian restaurant in Port Angeles?
  A. Spaghetti Bolognese
  B. Mushroom Ravioli
  C. Lasagna
Answer: Mushroom Ravioli

Who took Bella to Arizona when she was trying to escape the tracker?
  A. Emmet and Rosalie
  B. Alice and Jasper
  C. Edward and Charlie
Answer: Alice and Jasper

At the end of *Twilight*, where does Bella's step dad get a job?
  A. Florida
  B. Arizona
  C. Seattle
Answer: Florida

What did Bella Swan bid adieu to when she left Arizona for Washington?
    A. Her galoshes
    B. The sun
    C. Her ballet slippers
Answer: The sun

Name the place where Bella and Edward honeymoon?
    A. Isle Esme
    B. Honolulu, Hawaii
    C. Paris, France
Answer: Isle Esme

What does Bella want to name her daughter?
    A. Renesmee Carlie
    B. Carley Edwina
    C. Renee Marie
Answer: Renesmee Carlie

What is the color of Bella's prom dress?
    A. Burgundy
    B. Deep blue
    C. Hot pink
Answer: Deep blue

How does Bella describe the smell of blood?
    A. Salt and rust
    B. Sugar and spice
    C. No smell
Answer: Salt and rust

Name Bella's mom.
    A. Renee
    B. Elizabeth
    C. Makenna
Answer: Renee

According to *New Moon*, how long has Bella's grandmother been gone/dead?

    A. It doesn't mention how many years

    B. Six months

    C. Six years

Answer: Six years

What did Charlie give Bella for her birthday?

    A. Camera

    B. Photo album

    C. Purse

Answer: Camera

What does Bella tell her dad after she has a baby?

    A. That it is her baby

    B. That the baby is a baby vampire

    C. That the baby is adopted

Answer: That the baby is adopted

What does Bella always wear?

    A. A brown jacket

    B. A black coat

    C. A yellow rain slicker

Answer: A brown jacket

Twilight Saga and Beyond

Twilight won how many awards at the MTV Movie Awards?
  A. 5
  B. 15
  C. 1
Answer: 5

When were the MTV Movie Awards held?
  A. July 28, 2009
  B. August 9, 2009
  C. May 31, 2009
Answer: May 31, 2009

What does James steal from Waylon?
  A. Boots
  B. Shirt
  C. Jacket
Answer: Jacket

When did filming begin for *Eclipse*?
  A. August 2009
  B. Hasn't started yet
  C. December 31, 2009
Answer: August 2009

How many awards did *Twilight* receive at the Teen Choice Awards?
  A. 7
  B. 11
  C. 13
Answer: 11

When is Robert Pattison's birthday?
  A. May 13
  B. June 13
  C. September 13
Answer: May 13

What is Renesme's nickname?
A. Nessie
B. Bessie
C. Bellicious
Answer: Nessie

In *Breaking Dawn*, who was Bella going to hand Reneseme off to, to keep her safe from the Volturi?
A. Charlie
B. Renee
C. Jacob
Answer: Jacob

What two international locations did *New Moon* film in?
A. Canada and Italy
B. Africa and England
C. Canada and Spain
Answer: Canada and Italy

In *Twilight*, Bella goes shopping with whom?
A. Jasper and Alice
B. Jessica and Angela
C. Rosalie and Esme
Answer: Jessica and Angela

Who shows up at Bella's wedding unexpectedly?
A. Phil
B. Victoria
C. Jacob
Answer: Jacob

What burns in the microwave in the book *Eclipse*?
A. Spaghetti
B. Pasta sauce
C. Nothing
Answer: Pasta sauce

In the movie *Twilight*, what does Bella say the population of Forks, Washington, is?
    A. 3,113
    B. 3,120
    C. The population is only mentioned in the book
Answer: 3,120

What is an epigraph?
    A. A quote at the beginning of a novel
    B. A quote at the end of a novel
    C. An excerpt from the Bible
Answer: A quote at the beginning of a novel

What is the epigraph in *New Moon*?
    A. These violent delights have violent ends and in their triumph die, like fire and powder, which, as they kiss, consume.
    B. For God so loved the world that he gave his only son, that whoever believes in him will not perish, but have everlasting life. (John 3:16)
    C. There was no epigraph.
Answer: These violent delights have violent ends and in their triumph die, like fire and powder, which, as they kiss, consume. The original source is *Romeo and Juliet*, act 2, scene 6, by Shakespeare.

New Moon debuted in the United States on what day?
    A. November 20, 2009
    B. November 29, 2009
    C. December 31, 2009
Answer: November 20, 2009

Which of the Cullen clan is the fattest runner?
    A. Emmett
    B. Alice
    C. Edward
Answer: Edward

What location besides Port Angeles was used in the movie *Twilight*?
   A. Seattle, Washington
   B. Fresno, California
   C. St. Helens, Oregon
Answer: St. Helens, Oregon

According to Author Stephenie Meyer

What is the exact date Stephenie began writing *Twilight*?
- A. June 2, 2004
- B. June 8, 2003
- C. June 2, 2003

Answer: June 2, 2003

Coincidentally, Stephenie recalls that the day she began writing *Twilight* was also the day that what happened?
- A. Her children had their first day of swim lessons
- B. Her husband started a new job
- C. Her children had their last day of swim lessons

Answer: Her children had their first day of swim lessons

What inspired Stephenie Meyer to write *Twilight*?
- A. A nightmare
- B. A dream
- C. A dream someone shared with her

Answer: A dream

How does Stephenie describe her main characters in *Twilight*?
- A. She always knew they were Edward and Bella
- B. She initially named her characters Ronald and Alice
- C. She initially called her main characters he and she in the beginning manuscript of *Twilight*

Answer: She initially called her main characters he and she in the beginning manuscript of *Twilight*

What did Stephenie call her manuscript?
- A. It was always *Twilight*
- B. *Forks*
- C. *The Adventures of a Vampire Lover*

Answer: *Forks*

How did Stephenie arrive at the name Bella Swan for her main character?

    A. She had been reserving the name Isabella for her future daughter, but since her daughter hadn't arrived yet in real life, she decided to use her favorite girls name for the character.

    B. The name Bella Swan came to Stephenie in a dream.

    C. Stephenie's best friend's daughter is named Isabella.

Answer: She had been reserving the name Isabella for her future daughter, but since her daughter hadn't arrived yet in real life, she decided to use her favorite girls name for the character.

About the Author

Gina Meyers is best known for her popular culture television trivia and cooking expertise books related to the Twilight Saga and the iconic television show *Bewitched*. Gina's *Love at First Bite: the Unofficial Twilight Cookbook*, first edition, has been listed in *OK!* magazine's top *Twilight* merchandise must-haves. Gina's  *Magic of Bewitched* trivia books and cookbooks have sold over 3,000 copies internationally, and she was featured as the top *Bewitched* expert on the television show documentary *Fanatical*.

Gina has been a television consultant for *Popstar! Magazine* and Columbia Pictures Television, as well as *Nickelodeon Magazine*. She is a featured business expert at business.com and the *San Jose Cooking Examiner*.

If you are interested in the upcoming Unofficial *Twilight* Conventions, *Twilight* Cooking Events, and tours of Forks, Washington, e-mail twilightcooking@gmail.com or visit www.unofficialtwilightcookbook.blogspot.com.

Acknowledgments

Much love and thanks to my husband, daughter and son for their continued support, understanding, and sacrifice for my cookbook writing. Thank you dear husband David for being patient, for providing critical feedback on food presentation and for your excellent graphic design abilities in cover design and keen eye for detail and of course for your major contributions to this cookbook as well as our other book projects.

Special thanks to Lauren and Lucas for being my guinea pigs in the kitchen for trying most things that I created for this cookbook and for providing recipe name ideas. Thanks Lauren for being my hand model for the cover of this and my other books. I know as a teenager Lauren it isn't easy having a mom who writes all the time and sometimes about topics that hit close to home, I am just so proud of you for your creativity in ballet, your schooling and choir, keep up the great work! You guys are my life!!!!

Extra thanks mom for being such an excellent entertainer, hostess, and great cook. You have always shown excitement and passion in the kitchen, which luckily I have been surrounded with and continue to witness your wizardry in the culinary arts for most holidays and ones we make up. Of course thank you also for your organizational, teaching, command of the English language and interest in learning, all of these skills that make up you have assisted me on my life's quest of writing, teaching, and loving.

Thanks dad for being so much like character Charlie Swan, it wasn't long after reading *Twilight* that the similarities between Bella and Charlie and their father-daughter relationship mirrored real life for me and as such became partial inspiration for *Love at First Bite*. Also thank you dad for your sound advice and creative soul and spirit. Your writings and paintings continue to amaze and astound me and others.

Special thanks Nonie Julie for being the epitome of a great Italian cook. Your special Christmas dinners, homemade raviolis, torta, and special biscotti cookies are inspiration for many recipes found in this cookbook.

Extra hugs to my life long friends Dr. Christine Thai Dang and Jami O'Shea Smith (and their husbands' David and Tim) for always taking the time to support and participate in the book signings and the journey.

Thank you to friends that have uplifted and inspired me in my projects, specifically Sara Avena and Liz Longo. Also a warm thank you to my First Tuesday's group of ladies in Fresno, California.

Love and kisses to Aunt Denice and Uncle Gino (and cousins) for always being supportive, upbeat, positive and encouraging. A huge outpouring of thanks for allowing us respite in your Forks type surroundings over Spring break 2010.

Thank you to iuniverse for taking another bite at *Love at First Bite*. Thank you to Stephenie Meyer for pursuing her dream of writing and for sharing it with the world. And thank you to Twilight Saga fans for your interest in my original *Twilight* cookbook.

Index

Cocktails Index